The Archaeology Handbook

The Archaeology Handbook

A Field Manual and Resource Guide

Bill McMillon

John Wiley & Sons, Inc.

New York • Chichester • Brisbane • Toronto • Singapore

Library of Congress Cataloging in Publication Data:

McMillon, Bill, 1942–
    The archaeology handbook: a field manual and resource guide /
Bill McMillon.
      p. cm.
    Includes index.
    ISBN 0-471-55015-9   ISBN 0-471-53051-4 (pbk.)
    1. Archaeology—Field work. 2. Archaeology—United States—Field
work. 3. Archaeology—United States—Societies, etc.—Directories.
4. Archaeology—Bibliography. 5. United States—Antiquities.
I. Title.
CC76.M38 1991
930.1—dc20   91-10973

Printed in the United States of America

To Gerald McKibben, who often scoured the fields with me when we were youths,

and

To Jim Larick, wherever he is, for talking me into that first archaeology class

Acknowledgments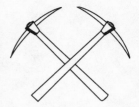

Acknowledgments are often overlooked as cursory thanks for people who gave invaluable assistance to an author in the development of a book. I don't want this one to be overlooked, for the assistance that I was given by the many people working in the offices of state archaeologists as I looked for resources to include in this book was not trivial. Without their efforts, Part Four would be much smaller.

I would also like to acknowledge all the authors of the 1950s, 1960s, and 1970s who wrote very useful guides for amateur archaeologists, work which I depended on during my years of development. Although most of those guides are now out of print, or are not easily located, they are the basis of this work.

And I must acknowledge my wife, who often comments to our friends that I never dedicate books to her. Although she refuses to do many of the tasks often attributed to writers' wives, such as proofreading manuscripts, typing, and being involved with the continuing development of a book, she has given me something much more important. She has worked full-time during my entire writing career so I have not had to worry about the financial insecurity that often haunts beginning (and even advanced) writers. I am forever grateful for this, Mary, even if I don't dedicate books to you.

Contents

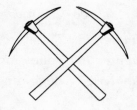

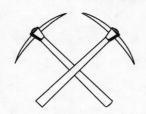

The Archaeology Handbook

Introduction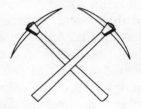

I, as a child, often scoured the plowed fields near my home in Northeast Mississippi for arrow heads and other relics left by the mound builders who had inhabited the region thousands of years before. More than once, my friends and I stumbled on a recently opened mound with hundreds, if not thousands, of exposed artifacts.

During my childhood, in the late 1940s and early 1950s, I knew little about conservation archaeology, or archaeology at all for that matter. I just knew the excitement of finding exposed artifacts. In fact, my cohort in many of those collecting forays still has the objects we found together, with labels telling where and when they were located. Little did we know we were beginning to develop some of the techniques used in archaeology. The recording of data about relics, and where they are found, is a key element in the systematic study of an excavation.

The memory of my excitement, felt when I found artifacts, led me, many years later, to include an introduction to archaeology in a social studies unit on early California for a class of fourth graders. I even went so far as to have the students plan and complete an archaeological dig in a corner of the school yard, where I had buried some contemporary artifacts. This unit went as planned, with great excitement on the part of most of the class.

An unusual interest in the subject was demonstrated by several students. Their interest was so intense they did a follow-up project on their own, with results far beyond anything I had expected.

A group of girls, using techniques they had learned during the unit, conducted an archaeological excavation at a mountain ranch owned by one of their families. Stories that a Native American village had once been located where cattle now grazed had circulated around the family for years, and, on a weekend visit to the ranch, the girls laid out a small grid and proceeded to excavate where they thought the village may have sat.

They returned, with great excitement, to school the next Monday, chafing at the bit to share their discoveries with me and the rest of the class. These included several arrow heads, a handful of pot shards, and an almost complete pot; all of which came from the test pit they dug during the weekend.

My excitement over their efforts quickly turned to concern as I realized two things. One, I may have led the students into unknowingly breaking the law, and two, I knew they had disturbed a treasure that could not be replaced—a previously unrecorded archaeological site.

This occurred in the mid-1960s, and what the girls did was not all that unusual for the time. Ideas about archaeology had changed little since I had been a child. Thousands of amateur archaeologists were still conducting unsupervised digs across the nation, giving little thought to the preservation of history. Most were collecting artifacts for their own private collections, but many were collecting them for sale to a fast-growing market for Native American artifacts.

These digs are deplored by professional archaeologists, because they know that an untold number of sites, with their stories of prehistory, are being lost as they are excavated without pertinent information being recorded in a systematic manner. Many of these professionals equate all amateurs with "pot hunters," and have pressed for new laws to prohibit amateurs from engaging in field work. Others, however, recognize the important role amateurs have always held in archaeology. Rather than condemn all amateur archaeologists, and deny them the privilege of working in the field, these professionals have tried to increase opportunities for amateurs to make important contributions to archaeology. Toward that end, field schools have been established where amateurs are trained by professionals, and given the opportunity to participate in professionally-run excavations.

Archaeologists have also pushed for more stringent state antiquities laws to help discourage pot hunters who continue to raid previously undisturbed sites, particularly those located on public lands. Federal laws governing the disturbance and collection of antiquities on federal lands had been on the books since 1906, but they were inadequate and poorly enforced.

A new movement began in archaeology during the late 1960s and early 1970s that also helped bring amateurs back into the fold; a movement which would come to be known as *conservation archaeology*. The purpose of this movement was to identify as many archaeological sites as possible, but leave them undisturbed unless they were threatened with destruction or were likely to provide new and significant information on the history or prehistory of the region where they were located.

The conservation archaeology movement and renewed interest in amateur archaeologists by professionals helped bring about a resurgence in amateurs' involvement. Today there are dozens of professional and amateur archaeological organizations where interested novices can go to obtain training, and literally hundreds of excavations ongoing around the world where they can go to participate in professionally supervised digs.

One thing changed very little throughout these decades. That was the fascination archaeological discoveries held for both amateur archaeologists and people with little or no archaeological background. When reports were circulated of new discoveries, whether they were in Greece, the Near East, Great Britain, or the New World, they captured the imagination of archaeologists and non-archaeologists alike.

Although professional archaeologists had often looked askance at the benefits of involving amateur archaeologists, or "volunteer" archaeologists, on important excavations, they could not ignore that amateur archaeologists were interested in assisting with excavations and had even been at the forefront of many archaeological investigations. It was also obvious that many important discoveries had to be attributed directly to the work of amateurs. Amateurs devoted long hours to their avocation even during the times that professionals were attempting to discourage such involvement.

Today, more and more amateurs, interested in working on archaeological excavations, are finding ready acceptance by professionals. One reason for this is the notorious lack of funds available to most archaeologists. The time has passed when native labor could be hired cheaply to do the intensive manual work required on excavation sites. Inexperienced volunteers are even cheaper than native labor, and can certainly do this work.

In addition, amateurs with experience are now regarded as capable of working with little or no supervision on some excavations. This is particularly valuable at sites where salvage work must be conducted quickly because of imminent land development projects. There just aren't enough professional archaeologists to salvage all the sites being lost to these projects.

This book helps novice archaeologists discover how they can become part of this increasingly popular avocation—a "how-to" and "where-to" guide that provides basic information about what archaeology is, how an excavation is run, what volunteers with limited experience can do on professionally run excavations, and the locations of excavations that use volunteers. In addition, it can be used as a handbook by people already involved in some aspect of archaeology who want a broader base of knowledge in the field.

There are some things this book doesn't offer. It doesn't provide an in-depth introduction to North American archaeology, although many of the organizations, museums, and archaeological sites included are located on the continent. It isn't an introductory archaeological text, or a history of archaeology; several excellent sources to these subjects are listed in the bibliography. Finally, it is not a comprehensive handbook for novice archaeologists who want to begin an excavation on their own.

In fact, I actively discourage anyone who wants to go "out on their own," because an archaeological site that is excavated with poor or improper documentation is a site lost forever. It is only with a thorough understanding of the how's and why's of excavation that anyone should undertake even a small dig without professional supervision.

Anyone who wishes to actively pursue work as an amateur archaeologist should have no trouble finding a position, whether for a weekend, a couple of weeks, or a couple of months, on an archaeological excavation, because of the many opportunities listed in this book, and the information from the section on how an excavation is done. Indeed, many positions can be found throughout the United States and Canada where amateur archaeologists fill in, as needed, on excavations, without ever going far from home or taking time off from work.

The first part of this book has an introduction to archaeology —its history and workings, and information about how to become a worker in the field, even with little or no formal training. The second part is a comprehensive guide to how a dig is conducted, from its inception to the publication of any discoveries at the site. The third is a short section on how to conduct an unsupervised dig if the need arises. The fourth part is a compendium that includes further readings on archaeology, names of museums with archaeological exhibits, locations of ongoing digs where observers are welcome, as well as names of travel agencies specializing in archaeological trips, field schools where anyone can learn how to excavate, archaeological organizations to join, and archaeological excavations in progress where volunteers are welcome.

First things first. Before further discussion on the role of amateur archaeologists in the field, we should define what we mean by *archaeology*.

Part One

An Introduction to Archaeology

Chapter 1

What Is Archaeology?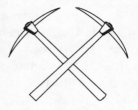

It is difficult to conjure up an image of archaeology without being influenced by popularized versions of archaeologists and what they do. Indiana Jones has captured the imagination of many people in the past decade with his esoteric discoveries and valiant battles against evil forces, but he is only the latest on a long list of Hollywood archaeologists.

For many years, the stereotypical archaeologist, as portrayed by actors, wore a uniform of a pith helmet, knee socks, khaki shorts, and safari jacket, while he supervised natives digging in the sands of Near Eastern deserts. Indiana Jones added other dimensions to this stereotype, ones that are just as misleading as those that came before his portrayal. Archaeologists are no more likely to become involved in wild, hair-raising adventures than an average tourist. Instead, most archaeologists spend their time excavating in isolated places, many in the United States and Canada—some of which are hot and dusty—and are excited by the discovery of artifacts that will add to our knowledge of human history and culture.

What Is Archaeology?

In a landmark decision, the justices of the United States Supreme Court once ruled that science is what scientists do. The same can be said for archaeology. To paraphrase the justices, archaeology is what professional archaeologists say it is, and most say it is a study of things that humans have made; a study conducted by using scientific methods to systematically recover material evidence of life and culture from past ages, and making detailed investigations of that evidence.

In other words, archaeologists try to reconstruct life and culture of past ages through the study of objects created by humans, known as *artifacts*.

This definition goes far beyond many popular depictions of archaeology, which often begin and end with the collection of artifacts.

For many years, however, that was the extent of the work of archaeologists. As the educated people of Eighteenth-Century Europe became interested in the classical worlds of Greece and Rome, they began to dig at sites in these regions in search of rare and wonderful artifacts. Most of these digs were little more than treasure hunts. Relics were collected, but no attempt was made to keep definitive records of the sites, or to determine much about the lives of the people who lived during the classical periods of Greece and Rome. Excavations were conducted, primarily, to enrich the private collections of the wealthy artifact collectors who commissioned them.

Today's archaeologists aren't just collectors. The information collected at an archaeological site about where artifacts were found, and what they were found in conjunction with, is often more important to the study of the past than the artifacts themselves. Instead of simply collecting artifacts, archaeologists attempt to determine the way of life of prehistoric and historic societies by studying sites containing artifacts these civilizations left behind. If they can make these studies without excavating a site they will do so, although many times they must unearth the artifacts to gain more complete information.

If a site is unlikely to provide new information about a region, and is likely to contain more of the same types of artifacts found by investigators in earlier excavations in the area, archaeologists will leave the site unexcavated. They will, however, make a thorough site survey so that future investigators will know what work was done at the site, and what is likely to be found there.

Some sites may contain artifacts that are in danger of disintegrating because of their age and composition. In those instances, archaeology is a science that must fight time—time that will destroy the stories from the past that can be told by the fragile artifacts.

Unfortunately, there is still a group of people who are only interested in collecting artifacts for themselves or others. Generally known as "pot hunters" by professional archaeologists and serious amateurs, these people have a long and inglorious history. Archaeological looting has been recorded since the times of the early Egyptian kings, and continues to this day. Many archaeological sites, particularly in Central and South America, have been thoroughly ravaged by looters in recent years, before professional archaeologists have had an opportunity to study the evidence from artifacts left behind by pre-Columbian civilizations—artifacts that tell wonderful stories of the rich and varied life of Native American societies before Europeans came to the New World.

According to customs experts, this looting of prehistorical sites, and its associated sales, makes the illegal marketing of prehistorical artifacts recovered from unsupervised excavations second only to drugs in international trafficking of illegal goods.

It isn't only pot hunters that have destroyed significant archaeological sites. Even the work of early American archaeologists was little more than glorified relic collecting. Much of the evidence of early life in the American Southwest was moved to Harvard University and other eastern institutions with a minimum of documentation of the sites where they were found.

The excavation of an archaeological site should be systematic, well-planned and executed according to the plan. Photo courtesy of the Foundation for Field Research.

The Evolution of Archaeology

Archaeology is a young science, and one that is still developing. In fact, in Europe archaeologists aren't even considered scientists. Instead, archaeology is considered a sub-specialty of history, and those who work in classical and biblical archaeology are often known as "prehistorians," and are as likely to be trained in art history or other history specialties as in archaeology. This is because the earliest European archaeologists were classicists and historians who had access to the written history of the regions that they were studying.

In the United States and Canada, archaeologists did not have written records, and those who wished to study the cultures of

In contrast to a systematic excavation, the pot hunter, *who is interested in only collecting artifacts, leaves devastation behind. Photo courtesy of Bob Parvin.*

ancient peoples of the region generally relied on techniques that came from a "sister" discipline, anthropology.

These differences in perspective between Old World and New World archaeologists have continued, but even though European and American archaeologists generally have different academic backgrounds, and concentrate on different regions of the world, they all have the same goal—they are attempting to reconstruct the life and culture of previous civilizations through the study of objects those earlier societies left behind.

As a result of this archaeological reconstruction of earlier societies through their artifacts, we have learned more, in the past century and a half since archaeology became a systematic field of study, about our origins and ancestors than the combined efforts of all previous generations.

Prehistorical Archaeology

The field of archaeology is roughly divided into the study of societies that existed prior to the earliest written records and those that existed after such records were kept.

Prehistoric archaeology is concerned with archaeological investigations of societies that existed prior to the beginning of written history. It depends, exclusively, on the interpretation of excavated objects, and their uses, to develop theories about how ancient people lived. As noted above, European prehistorians who work in the classical and biblical regions often have access to the written history of those civilizations to help them with their investigations of prehistorical cultures. However, much of their work is done on excavations of archaeological sites that date from even earlier times where no written material gives evidence of subsequent inhabitance, thus providing no clues about possible prehistoric activity.

Because of the great differences between the societies that developed during the earliest periods of human history and those that developed later, archaeologists have generally devoted themselves to the study of specific periods. To help define prehistoric sites and the periods they belong to, archaeologists have categorized Old World prehistoric sites into five distinct periods. These are:

Paleolithic Age.   The period beginning with the earliest chipped stone tools, which was about 750,000 B.P. (Before the Present). This date is being pushed back as archaeologists uncover earlier sites, but for the purposes of this guide 750,000 to 1,000,000 B.P. is sufficient.

Mesolithic Age.   The period immediately following the Paleolithic Age was characterized by the introduction of the bow and cutting tools, most of which were made of stone and bone. The beginning date of this period is somewhat nebulous, and is different for different regions, but is generally set at about 15,000 B.P.

Neolithic Age.   This period began about 12,000 B.P. in the Middle East, and is characterized by the early stages of farming and the making of advanced stone implements.

Bronze Age.   This followed the Stone Age (which includes all of the above three ages), and was characterized by the use of bronze weapons and implements, larger communities, and increased farming activities. Its approximate dates were 11,000 to 9000 B.P.

Iron Age.   This period began in Europe about 10,000 B.P., and was characterized by the introduction of iron metallurgy.

New World prehistoric sites generally do not extend as far back into prehistory as those in Europe and the Near East. Archaeologists have divided sites into only three categories. These are:

Paleolithic Age.   This period corresponds to the period of the same name in Old World archaeology, but does not extend as far back because humans migrated to the region much later. The date of the first immigrants to the region has often been limited to 10,000 to 12,000 B.P., but many archaeologists are beginning to question this dating, and suggest that humans may have been here considerably longer, maybe since 200,000 B.P.

Archaic Age.   This period is characterized by the collecting lifestyle adopted by the New World residents between 4000 and 9000 B.P. This lifestyle involved more dependence on collecting and storing food, particularly plants, than previous periods where hunting and gathering, with little storing, were dominant.

Woodland Age.   This period began about 2500 B.P. and lasted until about 1000 B.P. It was characterized by the development of pottery and ceremonialism.

Historical Archaeology

Historical archaeology begins, not with the beginning of written history, but with the beginning of written history in the region under investigation. In America, that means the investigation of life back about 500 years; in Europe, about 2000 years or so, and in the Near East, almost 8000 years.

Although historical archaeology covers a much shorter period of time than prehistorical archaeology, it is nevertheless a field that offers us great opportunity to further our knowledge and understanding of how our recent ancestors lived.

There is little difference between historical and prehistorical archaeology when it comes to the work performed in the field. Both follow the same methods, and both depend on the interpretation of found relics to develop hypotheses about how our ancestors lived. Where the two differ significantly is the starting point for investigations.

Prehistorical archaeologists have no written records to help them precisely locate potential sites. Instead, they must depend on other sources of information. Historical archaeologists, on the other hand, often begin their investigations in unusual spots such as local archives; building departments of cities, where early land records and deeds are located; and local libraries, where historical records are kept. All of these written records may include hints that help historical archaeologists pinpoint the location of potential excavations, thus giving us information about early life in locations around the world.

While prehistorical archaeology has been of general interest in America since before the time of Thomas Jefferson (who conducted one of the first systematic and documented excavations in archaeology), historical archaeology was of little interest until late in the nineteenth century, when excavation of colonial and Revolutionary War sites in and around New York City began. The growth of historical archaeology as a separate field of study in America was slow even after these investigations, but the field was given a boost during the Depression years as both the Works Progress Administration and Civilian Conservation Corps excavated Revolutionary War sites as part of President Roosevelt's public works' programs.

The National Park Service began an excavation of the Jamestown settlement in 1934, and historical archaeologists moved into other periods of U.S. history. However, the first course in historical archaeology was not offered until the University of Pennsylvania did so in 1960. By that time, the Jamestown project, which is one of the best examples of what can be accomplished using historical archaeological techniques, was well underway.

Colonial Williamsburg, Virginia, where excavation and restoration began in the 1930s, already had 400 different structures that had been excavated, with many restored, by the time that first formal course was offered at the University of Pennsylvania.

Archaeological excavation, restoration, and laboratory work continue at Williamsburg, and hundreds of amateur archaeologists have participated in this project in the past several decades. Today, the project offers several field schools each year where the techniques used in historical archaeology are taught, as well as many volunteer opportunities for amateurs with, at least, a minimal amount of experience.

Urban Archaeology

Even though historical archaeology is a young discipline, it has already spawned several sub-specialties. One of these is urban archaeology, which concentrates on conducting excavations in urban areas. These excavations are often hurry-up excavations, also known as salvage archaeology, where an attempt is made to gather as much information as possible before bulldozers and backhoes obliterate all evidence of earlier occupations of the sites.

Industrial Archaeology

Another sub-speciality of historical archaeology is industrial archaeology, which is very popular in the United States, Canada, and Great Britain. The industrial revolution that brought about great changes in British and American societies, as well as the rest of the world, is less than 200 years old, but many periods in its development remain poorly documented, if at all. Today, archaeologists are working on many sites in Great Britain and America where they are uncovering evidence of how the revolution unfolded in its early years.

The first industrial archaeology excavation was made at a site near Birmingham, England, during the 1950s, after bulldozers unearthed the remains of one of the first furnaces used to smelt iron with coked coal instead of charcoal. Given impetus by the discoveries made at that site, other excavations were undertaken to learn more about the various stages of the industrial revolution. Today, one of the most famous sites documenting those early years is at Ironbridge Gorge near Coalbrookedale in the Severn Valley of England. There, archaeologists and historians excavate new discoveries, restore buildings and furnaces, and operate the industrial museum that depicts the earliest days of the industrial revolution—a revolution that forever changed the world.

Underwater Archaeology

The newest sub-specialty of historical archaeology is the recently developed underwater archaeology. While much of the attention given to underwater archaeology has focused on the tremendous fortunes that are occasionally retrieved from sunken Spanish galleons found in the Caribbean, there are many other projects that utilize scuba certified archaeologists, both amateur and professional, to locate artifacts that add to our knowledge of various aspects of our history. The recovery of the Civil War era, ironclad ship off the Carolina's in the 1980s is one example, and work done in the harbors of cities in the eastern sections of both the United States and Canada is another.

Salvage Archaeology

While discussing urban archaeology, I mentioned salvage archaeology. Although it is true that much of urban archaeology ultimately ends up being salvage archaeology simply because of the pressures exerted by the impending destruction of sites by fast-moving construction crews, salvage archaeology may also be used at prehistorical sites. In the western United States and Canada, many such sites have had to be excavated under extreme time pressure as dams and freeways have been constructed in archaeologically rich areas.

Salvage archaeology, then, is involved with any excavation that must be completed under time constraints that prevent a systematic and thorough documentation of the site and the relics unearthed. While archaeologists are discouraged when they must conduct such digs, they are concerned that as much evidence as possible be salvaged from a site before it is completely and forever lost.

Archaeological excavation is not a simple matter of using earth moving equipment, whether it is a backhoe or a large shovel, to uncover a site. Even on a salvage excavation, archaeologists attempt to follow an orderly and systematic process. It is only with an understanding of that process, or of what archaeologists do in the field and lab, that amateurs can begin to recognize the importance of correctly conducting excavations.

Chapter 2

What Do Archaeologists Do?

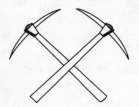

The artifacts uncovered during an excavation, and the corresponding data collected, are a nonrenewable cultural resource. Once an archaeological site has been disturbed it can never be restored to its previous condition. For that reason, all excavations must be undertaken with great care, making sure that as much data as possible is recorded about the site, and recorded accurately. If the data about the site is incorrectly or incompletely recorded, the historical value of the excavation will be minimal, even if most of the artifacts from the site have been preserved. There is no chance to go back and do it correctly a second time. The original context of the site is destroyed and can never be adequately replicated, even if the best excavation techniques have been used.

Since these archaeological sites are our only available source of information about prehistoric societies, and our only check against the written records of historical societies, every effort must be made to either preserve them in their undisturbed state, or excavate them in a systematic and scientific manner.

When archaeologists are able to conduct an excavation without the time constraints that salvage archaeology constantly faces, they conduct a site survey that delineates where they think an excavation should be conducted, break the area down into sections and subsections, and carefully begin to unearth the site. No move is made that isn't recorded, and nothing is uncovered that isn't thoroughly documented. An overview of the entire site is kept constantly updated, and all artifacts are labeled, and packed in labeled and protected containers for study in the laboratory. There, various techniques are used to clean and preserve the artifacts so they can be studied for age, use, composition, and other useful information.

Detailed information about each of these steps, as well as other steps in an excavation, is given later in this book, with discussion about which steps novices are most likely to participate in, and which are the province of professional archaeologists and their professional associates from other disciplines.

Amateur Archaeology

While it may appear from previous discussion that the role of amateurs in archaeology has been minimal, that is not the case. The early prehistorians who conducted excavations in Greece and the Near East may have been trained in art or history, but they were novices when it came to excavating an archaeological site. There were no written guidelines to help them conduct their excavations, and there were no trained archaeologists who could be called on for consultation. It was only through the trial-and-error experience gained from such excavations that techniques of excavating and recording began to be developed, and it was near the end of the eighteenth century that Thomas Jefferson, better known for his involvement with government and politics than archaeology, made the first systematic documentation of an excavation and noted what, today, is one of the most important facets of archaeological excavations—stratification.

Thomas Jefferson is well-known for his wide-ranging interests, and one of those was the excavation of pre-Columbian burial mounds around Monticello, his home in Virginia. While documenting the excavation at one site, Jefferson realized *where* artifacts had been found in the excavation was important. For the first time, he recognized that different levels, or strata, of deposits in the excavation represented different time periods in the development of the site. After this realization, he recorded the strata each artifact was found in to help him with his documentation of the site. This was the first known use of stratification in the interpretation of an archaeological excavation, and he was the first archaeologist to systematically report on the artifacts unearthed during an archaeological excavation through extensive documentation.

From those early "amateurs," archaeology has developed into, if not an exact science, at least a discipline that makes extensive use of scientific methods. However, the use of these methods is not limited to professionals who have had intensive, formal training in the field. Many advanced amateurs who have spent hours in the field or in the lab have an excellent knowledge of these methods and are actively involved in professional organizations. Professionals frequently collaborate with advanced amateurs to conduct surveys and excavations, and write reports on completed projects.

Archaeology has attracted the interest, attention, and participation of nonprofessionals far beyond any comparable scientific discipline, in part because there is such a need for personal involvement and observation in the field. This leads to large numbers of volunteers working on excavations, and doing the follow-up work of classifying, cataloging, and otherwise preparing data from artifacts and collateral information collected during excavations.

While many amateur archaeologists still simply "collect" artifacts, either through purchase, trade, or surface finds, more and more are becoming involved with scientific work in the field through discussion groups, planned workshops at field schools, and supervised expeditions, either near home or farther away. These amateurs are eager for information about archaeology and help in learning as much as possible about the field. Seldom do they engage in unsupervised excavations where they are little better than pot hunters and vandals.

There are still some amateurs who continue to destroy precious sites through a desire to "complete" a private collection. These people are easy to recognize if you are only slightly familiar with excavation techniques. If you see someone digging at an archaeological site who is not: taking notes, keeping records, making a careful analysis of each layer of dirt removed from the excavation, marking every artifact, taking photographs, you know that you have found someone who has very little background in scientific or conservation archaeology. If you see someone conducting such a dig you should immediately notify your local archaeological society or state/provincial archaeologist. They will follow up on your report to insure that the excavation is being conducted according to the legal requirements of your state or province. Most states and provinces now have strict laws about excavations of antiquities, although most do not forbid it on private lands. (Further information about the specific laws and regulations regarding antiquities and their removal can be found in Part Four.)

By properly obtaining and evaluating artifacts from systematic excavations, we have an opportunity to expand our knowledge of our ancestors. In this sense, archaeological sites belong to all of us. Pot hunters, private landowners, and many private collectors obviously see this differently. They are motivated by profit and wish to retain control of their discoveries or collections.

While private landowners do have a legal basis for this control in many states, my personal philosophy, which is also the position of most professional and serious amateur archaeologists, is that all archaeological artifacts, and all archaeological sites, should belong to all the people, and should ultimately fall under the supervision of some governmental agency. This means that few, if any, private excavations should occur for personal gain, whether or not they are on private land. If amateur archaeologists want to work on excavations, even on private land with the permission of the owner, they should do so in conjunction with their local archaeological society, state or province archaeologists, or local university archaeology department.

Who Are Today's Amateur Archaeologists?

In Europe, amateur, Old World archaeologists are likely to be professionally trained in such areas as art history, biblical history, the classics, or some other discipline that explores the early activities of humans. Their interest in archaeology simply rounds out, and complements, their other professional interests.

In America, amateur New World, archaeologists are far less likely to be professionally trained in any field that is allied with archaeology. They are just as likely to be teenage high school students or septuagenarian retirees as art history professors.

These amateurs come to archaeology with a wide range of interests and professions, but all have an unquenched desire to help preserve the sites of earlier societies, and advance our knowledge of how they lived their daily lives. They do this by participating in archaeological and historical societies, which can be found in almost every state and province in the United States and Canada; by enrolling in extension courses in local colleges and universities; attending a field school operated by a local or regional archaeological or historical society; or by joining any one of numerous excavation teams studying sites throughout the United States and Canada each year. They also travel to Latin America, Europe, Asia, Africa, and the Pacific to engage in professionally organized excavations.

Amateur archaeologists, pursuing these activities with the benefit of great enthusiasm for their avocation, have radically changed New World archaeology for the better in the past several decades. They have been in the forefront persuading state and provincial legislators to pass antiquity laws that help protect the remains of our nations' early heritage, and they have contributed time and skill to all aspects of archaeological research.

Active amateur archaeologists recognize that while excavating a site is exciting, much work must be done before an excavation begins. They also understand that some of the most important work in archaeology is just beginning when the digging stops.

Artifacts gathered during the excavation must be classified, photographed, sketched, and readied for study. After these steps have been completed, the data that has been gathered about the excavation must be reported to the public through monographs that are produced by local, state, province, and other archaeological societies.

Much of the reporting work that has been done by amateurs in recent years is of such high quality that it is accepted as the standard by many organizations in the United States and Canada.

Interested amateurs, both skilled and unskilled, are often used by museums in a variety of capacities. The museums use them as guides and docents, as guards, and as technicians who help catalog and maintain collections.

Amateurs contribute greatly in all of these roles to a field that is painfully short-handed and under-funded. Amateur archaeologists keeping their amateur status in mind, as well as their relationship to professional archaeologists, can find their avocation stimulating and rewarding, not only to themselves, but to archaeology as a whole.

Nothing can be more exciting than making a contribution to the knowledge of human history, and viewing a rare and delicate relic that will help make such a contribution as it is slowly unearthed by gentle and cautious manipulation of trowel and brush.

Before you can experience such a moment, however, you must know something about how an excavation is run, and the how's and why's of excavation techniques, and post-excavation research, used by both professional and nonprofessional archaeologists.

Part Two

On a Dig

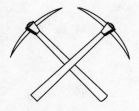

Chapter 3

Before You Get to an Excavation

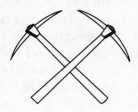

Many important decisions have been made, and steps taken, by the time you, as a novice archaeologist, get involved in an excavation. Many of these decisions are about how to proceed with the excavation, and how to staff it. It is important to you, and to the professionals and advanced amateurs you will be working with, that you know what work was completed prior to the start of the actual digging, and what decisions were made as well as why they were made. The success or failure of an excavation is often determined by the effectiveness of the initial plans of the expedition. You can become a more important contributor to a successful expedition by knowing as much as possible about the total operation.

A century ago, most archaeological excavations in the United States or Canada resulted from accidental discoveries of prehistorical sites, and excavation leaders had few guidelines to help them develop excavation plans. Today most excavations result from disciplined searches for sites that will furnish new information about the history or prehistory of a region, and expedition leaders have a broad base of formal methodology to guide them in their pursuits.

Archaeology is the study of all aspects of life of earlier societies, and an examination of a simple collection of artifacts left behind is almost meaningless. To truly understand the people who made the artifacts and gain useful information about how they lived, archaeologists must carefully collect and record all of the findings of an excavation. This includes data about where various artifacts were located, and their relationship to each other.

Archaeologists have developed a set of skills, methods, and procedures to insure that as much information as possible about the site being excavated is systematically recorded.

When you join an excavation, most of the behind-the-scenes work will have been completed and excavation procedures will have been carefully established. You must learn what your role will be in seeing that the expedition's goals are reached. You will also need to know what the other people involved in the expedition will be doing.

As a novice, you will most likely be assigned to a position as a digger's assistant on the excavation team where you will be supervised by an experienced person. You will need minimal training for the work in which you will be engaged, but the work will be easier, and make more sense to you, if you have some basic knowledge of what is involved with an excavation.

One way to obtain that basic knowledge is to attend one of the field schools operated by state and local archaeological societies, or offered, as a class, by a university archaeology program. Not only will this experience give you a basic foundation in the operation of excavations, you may also become certified as a field technician. The skills and knowledge required to gain this certification vary from field school to field school, but most schools require that students have, at least, the following knowledge before certifying them as field technicians.

- Understand the use of a grid in an excavation.
- Understand the concept of charting the location of artifacts within the squares formed by the grid, and be able to do so.
- Be able to excavate a square with the walls straight and the floor level.
- Recognize the categories of artifacts that may be uncovered at a site.

- Be able to map artifacts found within a square, and note features such as roots and geologic formations that may have affected the location of the artifacts.
- Use trowels and other tools to properly remove material while searching for artifacts.
- Screen materials that have been excavated.
- Label and bag artifacts with proper identification.
- Keep accurate and complete excavation notes.
- Clean and care for field equipment.

It isn't necessary for you to gain certification before joining an expedition because most expedition leaders expect to teach these skills on-site. However, they are always pleased when new participants have at least some idea of what is expected of them.

Although you may have skills to contribute to an expedition, others will have much more experience, and will hold more responsible positions in the day-to-day operations. After working on several expeditions, you will have the expertise necessary to hold some of the more responsible positions, and, one day, may even direct your own excavation.

 ## Administration and Staffing of an Expedition

Who runs an expedition and what roles each person on the expedition performs are as important to the ultimate success of an excavation as the down and dirty work of removing layers of sand and dirt to uncover artifacts.

A number of jobs must be done on every dig, and as a team member, whether experienced or novice, you will be expected to fill one or more staff positions. If an expedition is small, more will be expected of every staff member—if it is large, then there is an opportunity for each staff member to specialize in a specific activity.

While each expedition has its own organizational chart, the staff positions described below are typical.

Expedition Director

All excavations have a director. This position is usually filled by someone who is more experienced than other members of the expedition, and is either a professional or advanced amateur archaeologist who has worked on a number of excavations prior to becoming an expedition director. This person is directly responsible for the entire operation of the excavation, from obtaining permission to dig from the correct agency to the publication of excavation results. Very little is done on a dig without the knowledge and approval of the director.

Logistical issues such as housing, food service, and equipment selection and acquisition are also the direct responsibility of the director, although they may be delegated to other members of the expedition.

Field Supervisor

The field supervisor, also known as the chief digger, must be experienced because he or she directs the actual digging at the excavation site. This responsibility includes seeing that all excavated material is checked for artifacts and that all found artifacts are properly recorded. On a small project, the expedition director often doubles as the field supervisor.

Digger

A digger may be less experienced than either the expedition director or field supervisor, but should have some training or experience. This background and experience enables the field supervisor to give to the digger the authority to remove material from the dig. On small excavations the field supervisor and digger may be the same person.

Digger Assistant

The digger assistant can be a novice with little or no experience, for the primary duties of this position are to remove material under the supervision of the digger, take material to the screening area, and deposit screened material onto a material dump. Assistants also label artifacts and bag them for later study.

You will most likely begin your archaeological experience in this position. You will have little decision making responsibility as a digger's assistant, but will be an important part of the excavation, for you, and others with minimal experience, make it possible for an excavation to move forward at a steady pace. Some excavations assign two or three assistants to each digger, while others might assign only one assistant to every two diggers. This choice is simply the preference of the field supervisor and expedition director.

Recorder

Each digger should be assigned one recorder who is trained in proper recording procedures, someone who can faithfully record everything that occurs as the digger and assistant carefully remove layers of material. Recording is done in written and graphic format, and various forms are routinely developed to facilitate the process.

Photographer/Artist

If at all possible, every expedition should have a photographer and/or artist to document significant finds. He or she is responsible for accurately recording, by illustration or photograph, where artifacts were found and their relationship to other artifacts. The recorder may have this responsibility, but it is desirable to have another person handle it.

Novices who have either artistic or photographic skills are given particular preference by many expedition directors. Experienced draftspersons are often used to perform this function, and the function of assistant to the surveyor—who conducts a site survey prior to the digging procedure.

In addition, technical specialists, such as surveyors, are often used on excavations prior to the beginning of the digging.

There is no set or standard staffing pattern on excavations, so the positions described above may or may not apply to the digs you join, but most expeditions will have a similar administrative structure. The number of people used and their assigned responsibilities are based on the needs and desires of expedition directors. Several factors affect staffing patterns, including the size of the excavation and the experience of the staff. The smaller the site the fewer people needed on the site. For that reason, excavations in North America generally have fewer people than excavations in the Near East, where the sites cover a much larger area.

Fewer people are needed on a site when everyone is experienced, because the director and field supervisor do not need to keep as close an eye on all that occurs. With less experienced staff, supervision must be closer. Regardless of staff experience, nothing should be dug, removed from its location, sent to the screen, or recorded without director, supervisor, or digger approval. This approval process is important to insure that nothing is missed or discarded without being checked and double-checked, for once something is overlooked or incorrectly recorded it is too late to go back and start the process again.

Archaeological excavations are important, and precision is necessary to maintain a scientific approach. Discipline from the top down is needed to establish a routine that leads to proper excavation techniques and recording methods. This, in turn, leads to a well-documented excavation, the results of which add to our knowledge of earlier societies. It is for these reasons that it is important that excavations be well planned and staffed, and that all members of the expedition perform their assigned tasks in a conscientious manner.

 ## Work Is Not Finished When Artifacts Are Uncovered

While many expedition personnel limit the work done by amateur participants to the actual excavation, others use them to do important follow-up work such as cleaning, sorting, and classifying artifacts found at the site. Amateurs may also be involved in report writing.

Chapter 4

Eating, Sleeping, and Working

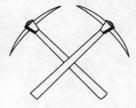

Those of you who have never observed or participated in a dig undoubtedly have questions that have little to do with the on-site work, but are about your basic needs. You will probably want to know where you will sleep, what you will eat, what kind of personal items and tools you should bring with you, and who is responsible for making all these arrangements and telling you about them.

You will probably sleep in tents and eat camp fare along with the rest of the expedition crew. However, a few expeditions, notably some in France that are excavating and restoring medieval villages, house their crews in hotels and castles and feed them in two-star restaurants.

These excavations are not usual, and may be worth joining simply for their room and board.

Almost without exception, the expedition director will arrange for your housing and meals during your stay at the excavation site, and will only expect you to bring your personal effects such as toiletries, sleeping bag, and clothing. Occasionally, a director will ask you to bring your own tools for use on the site. Most directors prefer to provide tools for your use.

Team members often spend their evenings listening to lectures about the site being excavated and general excavation techniques. Photo courtesy of the Foundation for Field Research.

Excavating Tools and Equipment

Although large amounts of dirt and detritus are moved during an excavation, little moving is done with anything larger than a long-handled shovel, and most of it is done with nothing larger than a hand trowel and medium-sized paint brush. However, some sites are so large, and buried so deep beneath the surface, that bulldozers, cranes, and water pumps are needed to remove enough material to begin the serious hand work required to preserve artifacts and note stratification. Excavations requiring such large equipment are rare, and few archaeologists, amateur or professional, ever have an opportunity to participate in them.

Participants on an archaeological excavation generally sleep in tents, and eat food prepared in camp kitchens. Photo courtesy of the Foundation for Field Research.

The standard tools and equipment that are usually used to excavate and record a dig are nothing more elaborate than those that most gardeners and home maintenance hobbyists are familiar with. The most commonly used tools for excavation are:

- Long- and short-handled shovels
- Various types of long- and short-handled hoes
- Pruning and root cutting shears
- Small and medium axes
- Heavy string
- Medium pocket knives
- Various shaped trowels with single piece blade and shank
- Standard-sized paint brushes

- Toothbrushes
- Tweezers
- Camera
- Assorted report forms

The report forms used for most digs are standardized. Many archaeological societies supply these forms for use by their members and associates. Some directors and field supervisors prefer to develop their own forms for each expedition so that they may record information unique to the site.

It is important that the recordings of information be made in a standard manner so that future investigators will have complete

Archaeologists use a number of common, household maintenance tools during an excavation including a whiskbroom, small brush, trowels, plumb bob, tape measure, string level, and small shears. Photo courtesy of the author.

Large tools such as a shovel, pick, small ax, and large shears are used on an excavation site to break up and move earth, dig trenches, and dig test pits. Photo courtesy of the author.

information about a site in an understandable format. This will allow them to easily comprehend what was accomplished on earlier excavations at the site, and expand those accomplishments.

On some sites more specialized and sophisticated equipment such as probes and various pieces of laboratory equipment will be used, but you are not likely to encounter this sort of equipment on your first couple of digs. Expeditions seldom have the funding that is needed to acquire this equipment, and those that have the financial resources to do so generally use paid staff rather than volunteers.

Chapter 5

Locating a Site

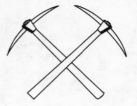

By the time you reach an excavation site, locate your tent, receive your job assignment, and pick up your tools and equipment in preparation for work, a lot of time and effort will have already been invested in the dig.

As noted earlier, many excavations in the past resulted from accidental discoveries of archaeological sites. This is seldom the case today, although there are some exceptions to this. A recent, accidental discovery was made by two college students, working as summer interns, responsible for tracking bighorn sheep in southwestern Colorado.

When Dave Merritt and Chris Kuzawa climbed over the rim of a cliff to follow some sheep, they saw mounds and vertical walls sticking out of sandstone next to a ponderosa pine forest. They wondered if they had stumbled on an undiscovered archaeologic site. The six-acre site of about 200 structures was subsequently documented as an Anasazi site and dated from about 1100 years B.P. It was undisturbed except for some evidence of "pot hunting" in one small area.

Because much has been documented about the cliff-dwellers of the Four Corners region, the region in which the discovery was made, the Bureau of Land Management, following good conservation archaeology methodology, made plans to map the site, but did not plan a large scale excavation.

One of the main reasons for the rarity of this type of find is that prehistorical and historical archaeologists in the Americas and Canada have developed extensive research techniques that help them locate potential archaeological sites of significance. These techniques are also important because there are thousands of archaeological sites around the world that could be excavated, but archaeologists don't have the time, money, or inclination to conduct haphazard excavations just because a site has been discovered.

The primary purpose of any excavation is to establish a sequence of cultures in a region, and to fill in gaps in the information that may have already been collected about the region. Archaeologists rarely go into the field to satisfy a base curiosity about a site and what might be found at a site. It is more common for them to become curious about a lack of information about a particular prehistorical or historical period and study research that has been completed about the period they are interested in. Only then will they attempt to locate a site that will be useful as a resource for filling gaps in that research.

To find a site that meets these requirements, archaeologists, both professionals and amateurs, generally follow a two-phase process. The first phase is preliminary library and map research. The second phase is the conduction of a physical survey of potential sites in the field.

Preliminary Research

The selection of a potential excavation site begins with the recognition that there are undocumented periods of a previously studied culture in a region. Based on knowledge gained from previous research about that culture, an archaeologist can narrow down the location of potential sites that might add new information about the period being studied.

This first step is the same for both prehistorical and historical studies, but the next step is somewhat different. A historical investigator will most likely begin to comb libraries, historical society records, government files, newspaper reports, and land records to gather information about the particular time period that lacks some specific information. An examination of these resources can result in an idea about the location of pertinent and important sites.

A prehistorical investigator, interested in a region in the United States, heads for another source of information—topological maps from the United States and Canadian Geological Survey. These maps cover every region of the United States and Canada, and contain some very important information for archaeologists who are looking for prehistorical sites. That information is the location of geological formations and natural features of a region. From earlier research about the region, the archaeologist will know where a society resided and can superimpose the location of previous excavation or habitation sites over the natural features shown on the map.

This will indicate what natural features exist in the area where people chose to settle—water, canyons, hilltops, forests, etc.—and a cursory examination of the map will show if there are any areas where these features exist that have not been excavated. If so, these areas have the potential for further investigation.

If no such sites are apparent, or all of the sites have been covered by shopping centers, subdivisions, and freeways, the region is not prime for a new archaeological expedition, and the investigator must look elsewhere in the search for new information.

If it appears that there are one or more potential sites, the investigator might look at both old and recent maps to gain further information about what may or may not have been built on the site, and search through the records of the local historical society to glean information, that may have been passed down through generations, about prehistorical settlements in the region. Using this information, the investigator can proceed and conduct a physical survey of the selected sites.

More frequently, investigators are utilizing one other procedure, aerial photography, to help them determine potential excavation sites. Aerial photography, and the more sophisticated satellite photography, reveal features that are often overlooked by observers on the ground. These features include shadows that appear at different times of the day, indications of varied types of vegetation that may be the location of buried walls, filled ditches, and overgrown building sites, for the land reflects all alterations to its natural forms.

This technique, especially using photos taken from satellites, has been particularly effective in locating ancient cities in Central and South America.

All this initial research can only direct investigators toward possible excavation sites. These possibilities must be verified by an on-site survey before any excavation begins.

Physical Survey

An on-site survey is the final step required before an investigator decides that an excavation is in order, whether the project is concerned with a prehistorical site or a historical one. Without an on-site survey, an expedition may dig for weeks without finding anything, simply because there may be nothing to find.

The techniques and the equipment used for an initial field survey are very similar to those used for an excavation, but they are less invasive. The primary purpose of an initial survey is to establish whether or not there is evidence at the site that will justify going ahead with a full-fledged excavation.

A survey team of three or four people—novices are sometimes used as assistants by the principal investigator—visit the potential sites noted on the topographical map used to locate the sites. They look for signs of unusual color or texture patterns in the soil, different types of vegetation growth, areas where there appears to be a break in the natural conformity of the land, and artifacts lying on the surface. Even the rawest amateurs are welcome on these teams because there is little damage that can be done at the site, and they can be used as recorders to note everything said and done by more experienced team members.

All members of the team can be more productive, however, by

Amateur archaeologists help map an archaeological site using surveying instruments such as this Brunton compass. Photo courtesy of the Foundation for Field Research.

having at least some of the basic skills described below. He or she should have the ability to:

- Interpret topographical and soil maps, and locate sites to the nearest quarter section on them.
- Read a simple compass.
- Recognize potsherds, bone fragments, and other artifacts and learn what to collect during the survey.
- Fill out a site form.
- Describe all artifacts discovered at site and label them correctly.

While most of the equipment used on surveys are low tech items such as compasses, trowels, and brushes, some professional archaeologists have access to high tech, electronic surveying equipment such as metal detectors, soil-resistivity meters, and photon magnetometers. These instruments can be of great help when searching for sites that may have few signs visible on the surface. Not many archaeologists use these, but those that do welcome novices who have access to the devices or experience in using them.

As the survey team is looking for the signs mentioned above, all team members keep careful notes that include information about the geographical location of the site; an identifiable name for it; the location within the site of geographical features such as types of soil and vegetation, creeks and other natural drainage systems, and changes in terrain; features made by humans such as roads, drainage ditches, fields, and houses; artifacts discovered on the surface; and abnormalities in the natural geography or vegetation that indicate previous human occupation in the area. Survey notes from all members of the party are combined in the final survey report.

While no laws directly prohibit archaeologists from making noninvasive site surveys while attempting to verify a site on federal, state, or local land, many laws across the United States and Canada prohibit any digging or collecting of artifacts on public lands. Some states even prohibit these on private lands. To ensure that they are acting within the legal parameters, archaeologists generally file a request before conducting a formal site survey on government land, or ask permission from the owner before venturing onto private land. Most landowners will give this permission once the purpose of the investigation is explained, and some will even give the investigator assistance by telling about the history of the region and artifacts that have been found nearby.

If the survey team ascertains there is sufficient evidence at the site to justify an excavation there is still a great deal of work the principal investigator must do prior to the first digging. If the evidence does not support an excavation, the team will prepare a report and map of the site, and file them with the local archaeological or historical society and state or provincial archaeologist so that future investigators can use the information gathered.

Chapter 6

Preparation of a Site

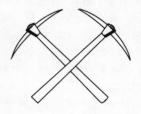

I have tried to make clear the point that all excavations are destructive, and the more complete the excavation the more complete the destruction. This must be instilled in the minds of everyone working on an excavation, along with the fact that the first time a site is excavated is also the last. This means that the excavation must be done correctly the first time. To ensure this, the expedition director must be very methodical in developing a plan that will enable the team to not only remove material layer by layer to reveal the sequence of stratification at the site, but to reconstruct, on paper and in theory, the information contained in the strata, both of which are destroyed as the material is removed.

Further, the excavation itself must be done in a meticulous manner. The site must be delineated to create a three dimensional view, and all information must be recorded in a way that reflects all three dimensions.

The first step in this process is often completed during the initial site survey before the first volunteers reach the site, but on small digs it is sometimes completed after they are on site. This step is to map the extent of the site, noting all natural features and features created by humans on or near the site. A permanent marker is planted in the ground near a corner of the site, and this point is marked on the map. This marker, often a steel pipe embedded

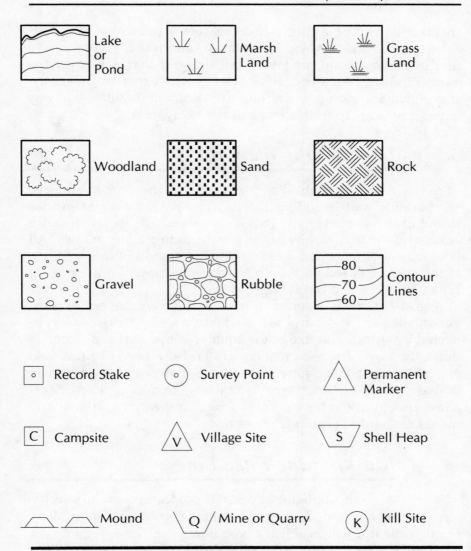

Lake or Pond

Marsh Land

Grass Land

Woodland

Sand

Rock

Gravel

Rubble

Contour Lines

Record Stake

Survey Point

Permanent Marker

Campsite

Village Site

Shell Heap

Mound

Mine or Quarry

Kill Site

These symbols and signs are the standard ones for use on archaeological maps and drawings. Standardizing them makes it easier for future investigators to interpret the recorded information about a site.

in cement, will give future investigators a point that identifies where the excavation was undertaken, and it is frequently used as the starting point for laying out the grid that will cover the excavation site. Amateur archaeologists with expertise in surveying and mapmaking or drafting are desirable additions to any expedition as help in this stage of the excavation.

Laying Out the Grid

After a rough sketch is made of the immediate area surrounding and including the excavation site, a more precise layout of the site is begun. This layout should include a distance scale, and the topography of the site, including contour lines. All later measurements and location documentation of artifact finds at the site are based on the grid and contour map of the site, so both should be laid out with precision.

A grid pattern is a set of squares that covers the entire excavation site. These squares are marked by a series of stakes connected by string. The size of the squares is optional and depends upon the size of the excavation site and the needs of the field supervisor, but most supervisors use squares that are between one and three meters (three to ten feet) to a side. These sizes allow enough room for workers to excavate within a square, and makes measuring within them easy.

Marking the Base Line

After the topography and natural features of the selected site have been recorded, and a permanent corner marker installed, the investigator will establish a base line for the grid. A compass, a supply of strong string, a long measuring tape of 25 to 50 meters (75 to 150 feet), some nails, a hammer or axe, and sturdy wooden stakes similar to those used by builders to mark corners on a construction site, are all needed for this step. A field notebook is also needed to record survey and grid information.

The base line generally runs due north and south or east and west so that any extensions from it can be described easily, and it can begin at the corner marker mentioned above, which then becomes the *datum point*. The datum point is the spot from which all measurements and plotting originates. Some field supervisors establish their base line outside the area to be excavated, while others use it to bisect the site, but either way the grid grows from it.

Once the datum point is located, a stake is driven into the ground to note the starting point of the base line. A nail is driven into the center of the top of the stake, and one end of a long measuring tape is hooked over it and the opposite end of the base line is determined. The direction of the base line is confirmed by using the compass, and a second stake is driven into the ground and a nail is inserted into its top. The tape measure is kept tightly stretched between the two stakes, and additional stakes are driven into the ground at a predetermined interval, say two meters, to mark off the bases of the grid squares.

Precision is necessary at this step because all future measurements depend upon the accuracy of the base line and the squareness of the grid that extends from it.

The rest of the grid is constructed by using either a level and transit or the 6–8–10 triangle geometric solution ($a^2 + b^2 = c^2$) to lay out two lines at 90 degree angles from each end of the base line. Stakes are driven at the predetermined interval along each of these lines the same as they were placed along the base line. The accuracy of the grid layout is verified by measuring between the stakes along these two lines. This distance should always be equal to the length of the base line.

If the base line is laid outside the excavation site it should extend past the estimated length of the site on both ends, and the parallel lines that extend from its ends should also extend beyond the site on both ends. When the grid is completed, it should completely cover the site so that all the work done there is within the grid and can be systematically recorded.

After the grid has been defined, and all the stakes have been driven into the ground, the individual stakes are given numbers. The first stake on the base line is generally A1, and succeeding

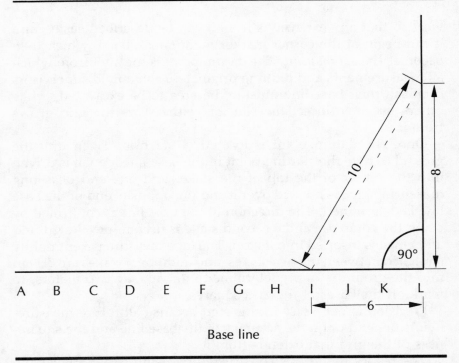

A B C D E F G H I J K L

Base line

The 6–8–10 method of determining square corners is often used instead of surveying a site. If precise measurements are made, this method is just as accurate as a survey and requires less expertise from the expedition team members.

stakes along the base line are A2, A3, etc. The next line of stakes are generally numbered B1, B2, B3, etc. Succeeding lines follow the same numbering pattern, which allows each stake within the grid to be easily cited when recording the location of a found artifact.

When the grid has been laid out and all the stakes have been driven and numbered (and lines strung to all the stakes), the field supervisor has the grid drawn to scale on paper so that the correct position of each natural feature and found artifact can be plotted during the excavation. Prominent natural features such as large rocks or tree stumps are plotted before digging begins, and the

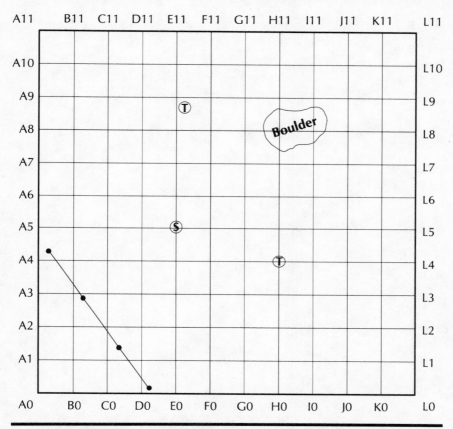

This is a grid map with all the natural and human-made features visible on the surface of the site plotted in the appropriate squares.

plotting of artifacts is generally done using rough sketches and field notes made daily during the excavation.

It is important that natural features found within the site, such as large boulders, trees, etc., be plotted on the grid plan before the excavation begins because they are often either so large that nothing can be excavated under them, or, if they can be removed, any artifacts found near them may have been moved during the removal process. All of these factors are reflected in the final

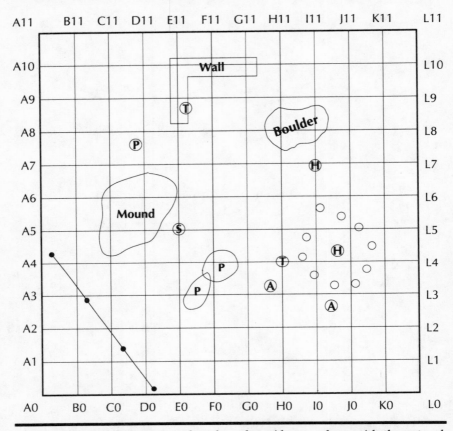

Archaeological features are plotted on the grid map, along with the natural and human-made features previously plotted. This grid map is continuously updated as more features and artifacts are located.

report, and the value of that report depends upon the care and accuracy with which the grid plan and site map were drawn, and the information about the artifacts was recorded.

Site Profile

The grid only establishes the horizontal layout of the site. The vertical, or topographical, relationship of the stakes and ground within the grid must be considered and recorded prior to any earth removal. Seldom is the land between two stakes exactly level; there are often rises and depressions on the site that are a part of the natural topography. These contours of the site, known as the *topographical profile*, must be measured and recorded prior to excavation so that the various strata of the site can be recorded accurately as the excavation progresses.

Contractors' levels and engineers' transits are used at this stage to take readings that will be recorded on scale or graph paper to develop a base line profile of the site. This profile will include information about each stake in the grid, and give information for determining strata levels throughout the excavation site.

Most novice archaeologists will not be responsible for the creation of site maps, grid layouts, and site profiles, although they may assist expedition directors and field supervisors in developing them. Advanced amateurs may need to utilize the applicable skills if they wish to make site surveys of potential excavation sites. A more detailed explanation of the techniques involved is included in Part Three of this book for those of you who may wish to conduct surveys and report them to your local archaeological or historical society.

Amateur archaeologists who have surveying and drafting skills are actively recruited for work as assistants to an investigator when he or she is conducting a site survey. Anyone with these skills who is interested in helping with site surveys can contact their local archaeological or historical society or college or university archaeology department, and their name will be put on a list of amateurs with special skills who wish to work on excavations.

With the completion of the site map and grid layout, the excavation is almost ready to begin. Many field supervisors, particularly of prehistoric excavations away from urban areas, add one other step before the actual work starts, and that is to conduct a preliminary dig near, but not in, the actual site to be excavated.

Chapter 7

Control Pits and Soil Profiles

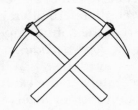

Excavation of an archaeological site is not just digging holes and hoping to uncover artifacts. Professional and serious amateur archaeologists know that they must measure and document every move they make, and that no move, from the first shovel of dirt removed from a site to the last bucketful replaced, should be made without a reason for making the move thought about carefully in advance of the action. Nothing is more important to the study of an archaeological site than the record of age found in the various strata, or layers of soil.

Fundamental to archaeology is the study of an archaeological site, and fundamental to the study of a site is the removal, layer by layer, of the soil covering the site, and the recording of any human-made disturbances discovered in the various strata.

Stratification is a geological term that is used by archaeologists to denote layers of soil, and any alteration or additions to those layers made by previous human inhabitants. By methodically studying the stratigraphy of a site, and interpreting data obtained from an excavation, archaeologists can learn a great deal about the groups of people that once inhabited the region.

Several things are important in the interpretation of the stratigraphy of a site. One is that the principal investigator be able to identify any changes in strata, and another is that all workers be able to assign any found artifacts to the correct strata.

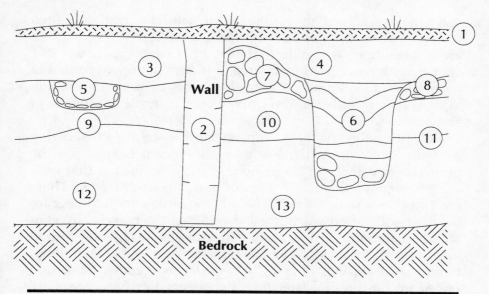

This is a rough stratigraphy profile of a site. The numbered features are (1) the surface layer, (2) a wall which is a complete interruption which extends from the surface layer down to bedrock, (3 and 4) the first stratum of the site with numbers for both sides of the interruption since the stratum may be from different time periods, (5) a hearth given its own number because it is a disturbance, (6) a pit which is a partial interruption that only extends part way to bedrock is also given its own number, (7 through 13) various strata with individual numbers for levels on each side of an interruption.

Control Pit

The first step in identifying the various strata of the site is to dig a control pit near the excavation site, but far enough away from the site to have little or no evidence of previous human activity. The purpose of this pit is to give the crew an idea of the natural composition of each strata, or *horizon*, of the surrounding soil. This will allow them to more confidently identify spots where humans have altered the natural soil deposit. Soil scientists observe that it is almost impossible for the natural state of deposited soil to be altered in such a way that a trained observer, such as an archaeologist, is unable to detect what has happened. Once an activity has occurred in an area, it is permanently recorded in the soil strata, and consequently, the history of human habitation in an area is recorded in layer upon layer beneath the surface of an excavation site.

Obviously, the first, or uppermost, layer of soil at a site showing evidence of human activity is going to contain evidence of the most recent activity in the region. Equally obvious is that each succeeding layer holds accounts of more ancient activity. There are exceptions which occur. There is the possibility that later inhabitants of the area disturbed the soil so extensively, by construction, farming, irrigation, etc., that the soil was literally turned upside down, or some natural event, such as a landslide or flood, moved large sections of land, thus evidence of earlier habitation ended up on top of a later one. Experienced archaeologists are able to determine if these kinds of disturbances occurred by looking at the surrounding soil strata.

While it is difficult to assign a definite date to a stratum, it is easy, and important, to assign a relative relationship among the various strata at a site. In this sense, each and every layer at a site must be accounted for in its relationship to other layers. Information about one layer is useless without information about the other layers.

A control pit, which need be no more than four or five feet deep, exposes undisturbed soil horizons of the area, and provides an immediate reference to the various levels, and what they look like, to all crew members. During the excavation, members can go to the control pit to check on the color, texture, and consistency of exposed horizons to compare them with those exposed within the excavation site.

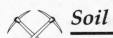 ## Soil

Since almost all excavations are made to uncover evidence that has been buried in soil (underwater excavations are an exception), it helps for any person involved in archaeological excavations to have some basic knowledge about how soil is formed and classified.

Soil Formation

Soil covers almost all the land surface of the earth and is formed by four different actions or elements. The first element is the raw material, rock; the second element is organic matter from vegetables and animals; the third is the climatic condition of the region; and the fourth is the passage of time. The combination of these four elements determines the types of soil found around the world, and soil scientists say the most important of these elements is climate.

There are three climatic processes that help determine the soil characteristics in a region. These are *laterization, calcification,* and *podzolization.*

Laterization occurs in hot, humid regions where most chemical elements, with the exception of iron and aluminum, are removed from the soil by heavy rainfall. The constant leaching of the soil and the high heat harden the iron and aluminum into laterite, which is a compacted, brick-like soil with low fertility. The southeastern portion of the United States and the equatorial regions of the world have large areas of laterite.

Calcification occurs in arid grasslands where there is not enough rainfall for significant leaching to occur. Calcium and magnesium remain in the surface soil, and large amounts of humus are added as a result of decomposition of the decaying grasses. The most fertile soils in the world are produced by these grasslands, and the *chernozem* (black earth) of the corn and wheat producing belts in the United States and Canada is a good example of the soil developed by calcification.

Podzolization occurs in cool, humid forests where organic matter decays slowly. This produces a thick layer of humus over highly leached soil. The resulting soil is shallow and nonfertile. It is found along the northern coastal regions of North America and Europe.

The soil deposits that result from these processes produce, at least theoretically, a soil profile. Seen as a side view, the layers, or horizons, of a soil profile extend down from the surface to bedrock. The first two horizons of a soil profile constitute true soil. These are often identified as horizons A and B, and correspond to the more common terms topsoil and subsoil. Horizon A, or the topsoil, is the dark, humus-bearing layer; horizon B is frequently rusty red or dark gray. This layer of subsoil contains accumulations of iron, manganese, and calcium that have been leached from the topsoil, and is often packed into a hard layer called hardpan.

Below the first two horizons is horizon C, which is not actually soil, but a layer of rubble and broken rock. This layer is generally lighter in color than the layers above it.

Horizon D is bedrock. It is generally found quite far below the surface in most of the United States and Canada; occasionally, it has been exposed and is the surface of some locations.

These layers may have been mixed, especially if the region has been cultivated for some years. In other regions, erosion has removed the top layers of soil so that rubble or bedrock is exposed.

It should be noted that these horizons, or strata, are different from the strata recorded in an excavation, although they may overlap to some extent. Soil horizons are the result of the four processes that form soil. Archaeological strata result from the human activity that has occurred in the region, and can be found within soil horizons or across them.

There are three, general classifications of soil produced by the natural processes described above. *Zonal* soils (which have two distinct zones or horizons, topsoil and subsoil) are the most common. They are found throughout the world, and develop from a well-balanced relationship between the amount of moisture precipitation and facility for drainage in the soil. Areas with zonal soil exhibit well-developed soil profiles with definite horizons of dark topsoil and lighter subsoil.

Intrazonal soils are found in swamps and marshes, and have poorly defined profiles.

Azonal soils are recently deposited soils found in river deltas, alluvial deposits in mountain regions of the western deserts of the United States, and active sand dunes. These often have no soil profile at all.

Within these classifications, soil is generally broken down into types. If a soil is composed of coarse particles and 75 percent of its mineral content is sand, it is a sandy soil. If it is composed of at least 25 percent clay (fine mineral particles), it is a clay soil. Silt is similar to clay, but contains larger particles, and soil that is at least 25 percent silt is silty soil. Muck and peat soils have at least 25 percent organic matter. When sand, clay, silt, muck, or peat are mixed together they form loam, which is the most common soil.

Archaeologists are interested in soil development and erosion since artifacts and other evidence of early human activity in a region are alternately buried and exposed by natural actions. These processes must be taken into account when interpretations of information obtained from an excavation are made. Most excavations occur in zonal soil, although many excavations made in the Middle East, the southwestern United States, and the badlands of both the United States and Canada encounter azonal soil conditions.

Chapter 8

Excavating the Site

An excavation site has been located, its likely boundaries have been established, a site map has been drawn, the site's topography has been charted, a grid has been laid out, a control pit has been dug, and the general soil types and conditions of the site have been defined. The next step is to begin the actual excavation. We have now reached the point where larger numbers of amateur archaeologists join an expedition.

Excavation comes from the Latin *ex* (out) and *cavare* (to make hollow), and it is a common term used by many professions. Archaeologists, however, use it to specify the methodology they have developed to uncover and study artifacts left behind by earlier societies. With occasional exceptions in geology and paleontology, archaeology, alone among the sciences, uses excavation as its primary research tool.

Excavation is much more than just digging a pit in the ground. Other writers have compared professional archaeologists' techniques with those of pathologists. In both professions, layers of material are carefully and precisely removed and a thorough examination of all removed material is conducted. While excavating can be compared to conducting an autopsy, there is one very important difference. In archaeology much of this important work is performed by amateurs under the direction of a professional.

This is not the case in pathology, or most other sciences, where almost all of the work is performed by professionals.

Most amateur archaeologists join an expedition during the actual excavation of an archaeological site. At this point, the myriad activities that have led up to the dig—locating the site, organizing the expedition, recruiting volunteers, and finding food, shelter, and money—have successfully culminated with a crew of professional and amateur archaeologists who are attempting to uncover evidence of previous human activity at a site that will add knowledge about how our civilization evolved.

Archaeology, like other fields of science, has three levels of study. These are observation, description, and explanation. Description occurs when archaeologists analyze the materials collected during an excavation, and explanation when they draw conclusions based on the analysis of the collected material. It is the first step, observation, that is central to all archaeological study, however, and observation occurs during the excavation of a site.

Digging Procedures

The start of the actual excavation at the site does not begin with shovels full of dirt being removed, but with surface debris being carefully scraped away and taken to a predetermined dump site. The location of the dump is very important, for it must be far enough away from the excavation site so that it will not cover any area that may be excavated, but close enough so that workers can transport material quickly and efficiently. The material transported to the dump is generally used to refill the excavation site after all artifacts have been removed, and all information about the excavation has been recorded. Refilling is usually required at excavations on state and federal lands and a stipulation saying so is frequently included on a permit issued to allow an excavation.

"Carefully" is the critical word above. Even the accumulated surface debris is searched for evidence of artifacts, and any arti-

All material removed from a site must be taken to the dump site where it does not interfere with the excavation. This dump material is located too close to the excavation. If the site extends out beneath the dump site, all the dump material must be moved again before further excavation can take place. Photo courtesy of the Foundation for Field Research.

facts found during this search are generally replaced on the surface where they were located before the surface debris was disturbed. The location of these artifacts will then be recorded on the grid map before they are permanently removed. Surface finds are frequently used as indicators of where the actual excavation will begin, because they are often a sign that other artifacts may be found beneath the surface.

Removing the Surface Level

After the surface debris has been removed and deposited in the dump, and all surface finds have been recorded, the

As the first levels of soil and debris are removed from a site, many surface finds may be uncovered. These are all replaced where they were found and tagged so that their positions can be drawn on the site map. Photo courtesy of the Foundation for Field Research.

first steps of the true excavation begin. The tools used for this step are determined by the type of soil at the site, the depth where the project director expects to encounter the first level of artifacts, and other factors that are relevant to specific sites.

In the United States and Canada, excavation at many prehistoric sites begins with workers using flat-edged shovels to scrape away upper levels of soil to expose the strata that contain evidence of habitation. At historic sites, and some prehistoric ones, workers

A team member examines a small find in one of the deep pits inside a grid square. Notice the paths between pits. Photo courtesy of the Foundation for Field Research.

are just as likely to remove this surface material with small hand shovels, trowels, and brushes because artifacts might be found near the surface. In regions where the soil is hard enough to be impervious to shovel points, a heavy pick is used to break up the surface.

This first material removed, whether it is thin enough to be removed with trowels and brushes or so thick that removal requires the use of a bulldozer, is usually a mixed mass that contains roots, grass, decaying organic matter, and objects that were deposited after the last human habitation of the site. Although little is likely to be found in this level, its profile is clearly recorded as it is removed, and its depth is noted in the field records.

This process must be done with extreme care so that subsequent strata evidencing human occupation are not disturbed. In this sense, the removal of the surface layer and succeeding strata is more akin to peeling away material than it is digging. The work required for removal of the material at excavations has often been compared to ditch-digging because of the amount of bending and loading involved in moving vast amounts of dirt and debris from a site, thus excavating is frequently referred to as "digging" and excavations as "digs."

The process could just as easily be called "peeling," and excavations could be "peels."

Exposing Succeeding Strata

After the first stratum containing evidence of human occupation has been exposed, workers begin the tedious process of removing soil from the grid area, little by little, until bedrock has been reached, or until no evidence of habitation can be found.

A general principle of an excavation using grids is that excavating is first done vertically, and then horizontally. This means that diggers first dig straight down, exposing the profile of lower strata within a grid square, until an artifact or other feature that indicates human occupation is encountered. When a feature is located excavation proceeds horizontally across the square to expose the totality of the feature as defined by the grid square.

These volunteers carefully remove a large artifact that has been strengthened with plaster of Paris. The artifact was left in place within the grid as it was being strengthened. Photo courtesy of Earthwatch and was taken by Thomas Stone.

While the particular location where the first digging is done may be chosen arbitrarily anywhere within the grid pattern, the field supervisor may choose to dig a test trench across several grid squares where evidence indicates there may be artifacts or other feature. This trench is also used to establish a profile of the various strata at the site.

Field supervisors will sometimes use the *vertical-face method* of excavation. With this method, an area somewhat larger than a grid square is designated, and the entire surface of that area is excavated through the top strata. This process is particularly advantageous when the site contains large, spread out features such as broad floors or ceremonial sites. A field supervisor may also switch to the vertical-face method when such a feature is uncov-

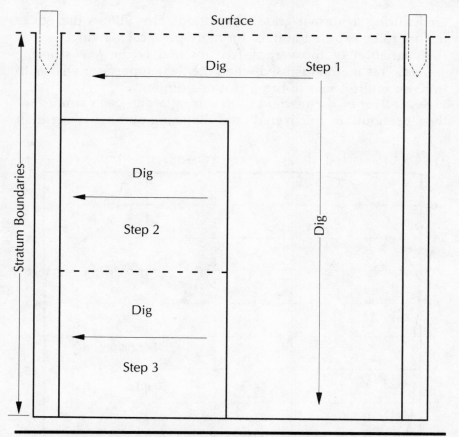

The first steps in excavating a grid square follow the illustration. Unless
an artifact is encountered, the first layer of the stratum is removed across
the entire grid. Approximately one half of the grid is excavated down to
the next stratum, and then the remaining half is excavated in layers. If an
artifact is encountered at any spot, the grid square—and any adjoining
squares in which the artifact might protrude—is excavated down to the
level of the artifact.

ered during a normal gridding method. This allows the entire feature to be exposed at once for more practical viewing.

A variation of the vertical-face method is the *level-stripping method*. This method is used when the field supervisor wishes to uncover entire levels of the site at one time.

Regardless of the method used during a dig, each stratum of the site should be uncovered carefully using nothing larger than

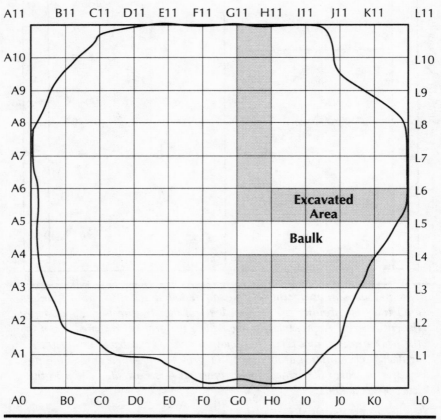

This grid layout illustrates how a baulk, or path, is left during an excavation. This area is used to move through the excavation area without harming artifacts or disturbing the strata.

a trowel or short-handled hoe, and no more than a one-half inch of material should be removed at a time. At times, particularly when a number of artifacts have been uncovered, whiskbrooms and other small tools are used to avoid disturbing or destroying artifacts. It should be noted that the trowel and short-handled hoe are not used as digging tools at this stage. Instead, they are used to scrape material from the surface. The reason for removing the soil in this manner is to uncover, but not move or damage, artifacts. Since many artifacts will be small, fragile, and fragmented, it is best to always assume that any object you may encounter will be easily disturbed.

As material is removed, the digger sweeps it into a dust pan and carefully sifts through it. After the material has been sifted by hand, it is placed in a bucket or other container that is easily transported. The filled container is taken to the screening area where the material will be resifted through a fine screen to isolate any small artifacts that may have been missed by hand sifting.

Keeping the Squares Square

It is important for precise measurements and records to be kept of the location where an artifact is uncovered. This location must be recorded in three dimensions, which means that not only must it be measured from the corners of the square being excavated, but its depth in the current stratum must also be measured.

To ensure this accuracy, all sides of the square must be kept perfectly vertical and all bottoms must be level and horizontal. The sides enable diggers to see and read the stratification, and the level, horizontal bottoms facilitate accurate depth measurements.

The field supervisor spends considerable time helping diggers maintain accurate measurements, because even the simplest artifact uncovered might turn out to be vital to the process of reconstruction of a site, and its precise location and relationship to other artifacts is important.

These archaeologists are using the vertical-face method for uncovering a site. Note that they are using circles rather than square grids. Photo courtesy of Earthwatch and taken by Sarah Nelson.

 ## Removing Material to the Screening Area and Dump

On a small site, it is relatively easy to move material from an excavated square to the screening area without disturbing the exposed site. A bucket of the removed material can be handed to an assistant digger standing in an unexcavated area outside the square, who can then carry it to the workers doing the screening. The material can be taken from there to the dump.

This removal becomes more of a problem on a large site, as does the movement of workers from one part of the excavation to another. To resolve this problem, field supervisors have work-

It is important to take accurate measurements of the depths of the strata, which is what this dig supervisor is doing. Photo courtesy of the author.

ers leave one-half to one meter of soil undisturbed on each interior side of the grid square. When two adjacent squares are being excavated simultaneously this leaves a wall one to two meters in width, which serves as a passageway for workers moving across the site. The width of the wall prevents the edges of the excavated area from caving in from the movement of the workers.

Screening

Theoretically, nothing should ever be removed from the site before all information about it and its relationship to other objects has been recorded, the artifact is photographed *in situ*, and its location is noted on the grid layout. In practice, however,

This team member is scraping surface material away by using the side of her trowel. The trowel is seldom used as a digging tool. Photo courtesy of Earthwatch and taken by Robert Angell.

there are occasions when artifacts are found in great quantity and their specific location when found isn't critical to the excavation, or when artifacts are so small that they are easily missed even by hand sifting. On those occasions, work is speeded up dramatically by the use of a screen.

On most digs there is a central screening area where assistants bring material from excavated squares. There, a crew of workers sift the material through a mesh that can vary from one-half inch to the very fine mesh used for window screens. The size of the openings in the mesh is determined by the size of the artifacts that are most likely to occur at the site.

This mesh is framed to form a screen that may be as small as twelve by eighteen inches—for use as a hand sieve—or as large as three feet by five feet. The larger screens are generally mounted

All soil and other material removed from the excavation is screened for small artifacts before being taken to the dump area. Photo courtesy of author.

on legs that elevate them to waist height, and workers rock them back and forth to sift the excavated material. As the dirt and small debris sifts through the screen artifacts are left on top.

Any artifacts that are left on top of the screen are labeled and placed in bags that are also labeled to identify the square and stratum where the contents were found. The bags are put aside for further study.

Chapter 9

Excavation Problems

Careful diggers soon get the feel of the soil being removed, and notice a change in the texture or structure of the soil that indicates the presence of an artifact. When there is this initial sign of the presence of an artifact, the use of any metal tools terminates immediately, and the digger begins to clear the dirt and debris with a brush. At this stage, the digger must remain alert for further signs of even the smallest micro-artifacts (those less than an inch long), as well as larger objects.

When an artifact is uncovered, any exposed part of it should be cleaned of dirt, and a search should begin in the soil surrounding it for other artifacts. If the first find is obviously a sherd (a piece of broken pottery) there is a strong possibility that other pieces are nearby. No attempt should be made to move the artifact until the field supervisor has been notified and had a chance to scrutinize the find.

After the field supervisor has been notified, and has examined the artifact, no further digging is done until a report is made of the find that includes a description of it, a sketch showing its location and appearance, the identity of the digger who found it and the supervisor, and its precise location measured by applying the surveying techniques being used on the excavation.

Only after all of that has been completed will the artifact be

All small artifacts are inspected, labeled, and then placed in a small container. The container is also labeled to ensure that the artifacts are not misplaced. Photo courtesy of the author.

Many archaeologists use small paper bags for containment of the small artifacts. Photo courtesy of the author.

carefully removed from the soil, and placed in the digger's find tray with the write-up described above.

Not all objects uncovered during an excavation will be artifacts. Found objects will fall into one of two categories: *artifacts*, which are human-made, and *natural objects*, which are not. Although natural objects are not collected, their location and description are often noted in the daily report. All artifacts, whether large or small, significant or insignificant, are collected and recorded by the process noted above.

While artifacts can range from micro-artifacts that are less than an inch long to pyramids and large structures, they are all one of two types. They are either *additive* or *subtractive* artifacts. A subtractive artifact is one which was formed by altering a base material such as stone or wood. However, the identity of the original material is maintained in the artifact. An arrow head is an example of a substractive artifact. An additive artifact is one which was formed by one or more basic materials, but the end product bears no resemblance to the basic materials. Pottery products are examples of additive artifacts.

Archaeologists would be very happy if all artifacts were uncovered in the simple manner described above, but it doesn't happen that way very often. Seldom are the strata of a site uninterrupted throughout the grid, and just as seldom are sites free of major obstacles such as trees and large boulders that hinder the removal and recording of artifacts. In fact, archaeologists recognize that few excavations are straightforward, and anticipate several types of problems that are common to excavations.

Excavation Problems

Basic to the study of any excavation is the study of its stratigraphy, and most of the problems that archaeologists expect to encounter during a dig involve disruption of the stratigraphy at the site. These problems form three groups. These are distortions, interruptions, and disturbances.

Distortions

Levels, or strata, aren't necessarily level. A host of factors can occur during the deposition of material at a site, as well as after the initial deposition, that may cause strata to disappear in one area of a site and reappear farther along at a different distance from the surface, thereby confusing those excavating a site. At many sites, a particular stratum may not cover the entire area, or even an entire square. It is only through clearing each grid square

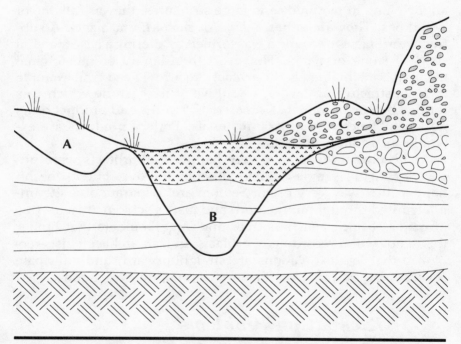

Distortions are the result of natural or human activities that occurred while or after the site was first occupied, but prior to the beginning of the excavations. These can be landfills (A) where habitants leveled out a depression by filling it with surrounding soil; dumps (B) where habitants filled in depressions or holes with detritus; or landslides and other earth movement (C) that tipped or covered strata with new material that distort or mix the earlier strata.

carefully and noting changes in strata that errors in dating and placement of artifacts can be avoided.

Cave-ins, floods, land slides, and other natural phenomena that occurred during and after the deposition of the strata may have distorted the stratigraphy of a site. Likewise, remnants of human activity such as dumps or middens from various periods of habitation during or after the deposition of the various strata can cause confusion for investigators. At some sites, uneven land forms may have been filled in to make the land level. All of these activities present problems when the stratigraphy of a site is interpreted, at least until all of the distortions are completely excavated and recorded. Great care must be used when attributing finds to various strata at a site where distortions have been discovered. It is easy to make extreme errors of judgement when the placements of the finds to specific strata are made if the distortions aren't correctly accounted for.

Interruptions

During the removal of material in a horizontal strata, large objects may appear which will interrupt the progress of the excavation. These can be natural objects such as large stones or boulders, roots from nearby trees, or the remains of fallen timbers, or they can be human artifacts such as walls, wells, and post holes.

The strata may be interrupted vertically by the objects, thus making it difficult to interpret the relationship of the strata on either side of the interruption. If this happens, a careful examination of the entire situation must be made before the relationships of various strata can be established. Field supervisors generally give strata on opposite sides of an interruption separate identification numbers until an uninterrupted strata crosses horizontally beneath the interruption. This is done because strata that appear similar may prove to be from different periods, and artifacts found on opposite sides of the interruption will be differentiated, thus avoiding confusion that might otherwise occur during later study.

A good example of this is a wall of a building, where artifacts

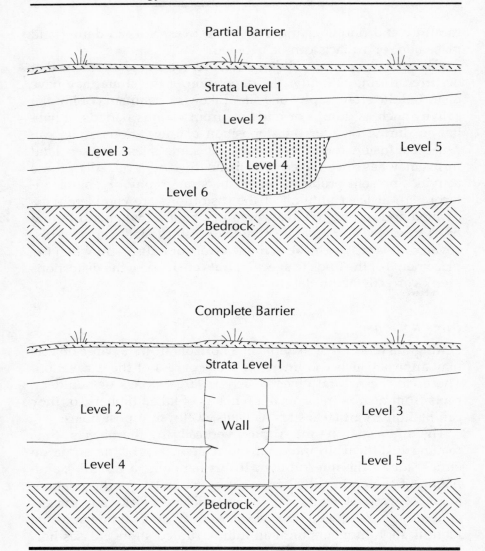

Partial and complete barriers may be found during an excavation. The partial barrier is a pit that extends completely through at least one level and into another, and the complete barrier is a wall that extends down to bedrock or sterile soil, completely dividing all strata below its top level.

After the floor of this pit house was reached, investigators began to remove all of the material, one layer at a time, from the entire area inside the pit house boundaries. This is vertical-face stripping. Photo courtesy of the Foundation for Field Research.

found on one side of the wall may be of a significantly different date than artifacts found right on the other side of the wall in strata the same distance from the surface.

Vertical interruptions, such as walls and wells, may extend all the way to the bottom strata of a site, therefore requiring identification of a large number of different strata. Rocks, boulders, timbers, and roots, on the other hand, are generally partial interruptions, and the strata that pass under the obstacles regain their continuity.

Several important notes should be made about human-made interruptions such as walls, post holes, and wells. Walls are not just built on the surface. They frequently have a foundation buried in the ground as a support for the superstructure. As the foundation trench was dug, and subsequently, soil placed around the base of the foundation, the site stratigraphy in the immediate vicinity of the wall and foundation was altered. One result of this alteration is the need for caution when recording the location and strata of any artifacts located near such interruptions. The horizontal continuity of surrounding strata is seldom clear. The area of the interruption and surrounding soil must be considered a separate strata, and artifacts found in this area should be assigned to different strata from those found just short distances away.

Disturbances

The major difference between interruptions and disturbances is that interruptions are more obviously solid in nature, thereby forming a barrier that breaks strata, while disturbances may be more casual interruptions of strata that do not completely break the continuity of the strata. These interruptions can be caused by the existence of various types of pits (storage, burial, etc.), trenches for post holes and foundations, natural occurrences such as stream cuts and washouts, or a variety of other human or natural activities. All of these interruptions have one thing in common. Because of their nature, later material could have become interwoven with earlier material, thereby moving artifacts from their original strata to strata reflecting a different period.

Many disturbances can be easily recognized when their surfaces are exposed in a stratum, but some are more subtle and present difficulties to excavators. Disturbances such as hearths can be recognized by changes in the soil color; holes that have been dug and refilled are recognized by changes in soil hardness; and natural activities such as floods and cave-ins can be identified by changes in the consistency of the soil.

In all of these disturbances more recent artifacts can suddenly be mixed with earlier ones, or vice versa, and all persons working at the disturbed area must become extremely careful. The best method to use when there is a discovery of a disturbance is to excavate around it, leaving enough soil to isolate the disturbance

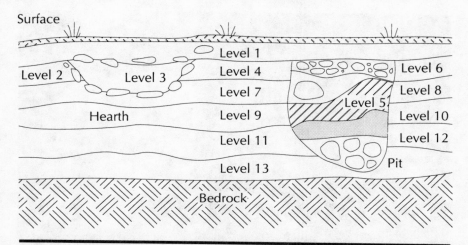

Hearths are disturbances that generally affect only one or two strata of an excavation. Pits can be either disturbances or interruptions, according to how deep they are and how extensively they interfere with various strata.

from the surrounding strata. The disturbance is excavated later, and treated as a separate stratum. This allows the dating of artifacts uncovered in the disturbance to be judged more accurately.

Since strata are always dated according to the latest material found in them, rather than the earliest, artifacts recovered from disturbances are less likely to be given too early a date if the area has been adequately isolated during the excavation of the surrounding strata. If the disturbance is not adequately isolated, it is possible for artifacts to be mixed with earlier ones from the surrounding strata, and consequently be attributed to an earlier period than they should be.

The problems discussed above are frequently encountered during excavations. All workers must be aware of them, and of their importance to the final interpretations of the excavation. In one sense, though, disturbances are what excavation is about. Theoretically, the purpose of excavation is to find disturbances, though we generally call them artifacts and features. These can

Some excavations take place in cold, wet locations instead of hot, dusty ones. The site director holds an artifact that was recovered from this obviously rich site. Photo courtesy of Earthwatch and taken by Suzi Moore.

be any remains of human activity, from small, fragile sherds to large buildings. The larger artifacts (hearths, pits of various types, post holes, foundations for buildings, burials, etc.), are generally referred to as excavation features. They present to the diggers somewhat different problems than those related to the smaller artifacts.

Chapter 10

Excavation Features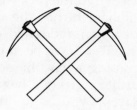

Most excavations result in an encounter by the crew with one or more of the "standard" features that are common to archaeological sites. These features are hearths, pits of various types, post holes or molds, mounds or earthworks, buildings, and burials. Each of these features presents diggers with a special situation that requires different techniques and precautions. Amateurs are frequently asked to deviate from their relatively straightforward excavation tasks when one of these features is encountered, or an encounter is anticipated.

Hearths

Hearths are found at archaeological sites in all areas of the world, and are the most common feature denoting human occupation. Humans have used fire for thousands of years, and for most of those years they built fires in simple, shallow pits. They cooked in the pits and gathered around them for warmth. Many artifacts were left around these gathering places, and great care is necessary when excavating the areas surrounding an uncovered hearth. Cooking utensils, eating utensils, and food remains are likely to be discovered.

Hearths are relatively easy to identify since the fires will have discolored the rocks used to line the fire pit, and charcoal remains will have turned the soil beneath the hearth area dark. When you encounter reddened or blackened soil or rocks in an area suspected to have been occupied for some period, you should stop scraping away the soil and investigate the immediate area for further signs of a hearth. Leave any stones and discolored soil in place as you use a brush to sweep away loose soil and then use a pointed implement to probe into lower levels for more stones.

When you have located the hearth, expose the top completely by brushing away all the soil, watching for any micro-artifacts. The hearth itself may be no more than a shallow basin filled with ash and charcoal, or it may be a stone-lined basin filled with fire remains.

No more excavation should be done until the size, shape, and location of the hearth is recorded. After all sketches and measurements have been made and photos taken, the interior of the hearth itself is excavated. The field supervisor will probably instruct you to remove the material from one side of the hearth, leaving the other half intact to provide a vertical profile of the deposits. Charcoal samples are generally removed if there are any found. These will indicate the kind of wood used in the fires and give investigators an idea of the plant life of the period.

After the hearth itself has been excavated, and all artifacts recorded, the area immediately adjacent to it is excavated, with particular attention given to the possibility of finding broken cooking and eating utensils, as well as carbonized food remains and bones; all of which will provide information about the eating habits of the people who inhabited the site.

Pits

Pits are the next most abundant feature uncovered in archaeological excavations. These are holes in the ground that were either intentionally dug, and then filled in with rubbish or other debris, or were natural holes that served as receptacles for the detritus of early residents. Either way, they represent a major disturbance in the strata of a site.

I described fire pits, or hearths, above, and mentioned that they were shallow depressions in the ground that were generally limited to one stratum. Other pits may extend down through a number of strata, and may be difficult to distinguish from surrounding soil. One indication of a pit may be darkened soil, either caused by charcoal left from early fires or by decayed material that was tossed into the pit. Another indication may be slight variations in soil color and texture caused by the variety of refuse material thrown into the pit by early users, or by the disturbance of the surrounding soil horizons when the pit was dug.

Pits were also used as storage areas, and the remains of the materials that were stored are frequently important in determining various aspects of the lives of the people who lived at the site.

There are several techniques that can be used to excavate a pit site. The top of the pit should be exposed and recorded in much the same manner as with hearths.

One technique is to leave the pit undisturbed, and to excavate the surrounding material through the various strata until only the pit, with a thin shell of undisturbed material surrounding it, is left. This is best if the pit is small, and only extends through one or two strata.

If the pit is large, and appears to extend down through a number of strata, it should be excavated in its entirety before the surrounding material is removed. If it is large enough, the pit can be dug in quadrants, or quarters, with two alternate quarters removed. Otherwise, one whole side of the pit should be excavated, with the other left to expose the strata of material that was deposited over a period of time. Both techniques will expose the profile of the pit, and give the investigator a good sample of the types of artifacts that are to be found in the pit, as well as an indication of the growth and evolution of the society that occupied the site.

One caution about pits is that artifacts within a pit may have been disturbed during the various periods of human occupation, and intermingled with artifacts from earlier or later periods. An

Pits, post molds, and hearths are excavated completely before the area surrounding them is excavated. This semi-subterranean house has an abundance of these features. Photo courtesy of Earthwatch and taken by Gary Crawford.

experienced investigator will generally be able to determine if this is the case, and will be able to avoid assigning artifacts to too early a period.

Whether one technique is used or the other, a pit is considered a stratum by itself, and the material within a pit is assigned additional strata designations as needed.

Post Molds

Wood has been used as a building material for a very long time in all regions where it is plentiful, and since organic matter decays very rapidly in many parts of the world (it will decay completely within five years in some regions), archaeologists often encounter sites where certain features involve the remains of decayed wood. The most common of these features are post molds, or holes.

Whenever wood has been used as a post that was driven or set into the ground, a record of the post, in the form of a cast or mold, remains for an indefinite period until it is disturbed by an excavation of some sort. The soil around posts is packed so that it will remain firm and hold the post upright, and this packed area retains the shape of the post long after all of the wood has rotted. In addition, it generally will have a slightly different color and texture than the soil surrounding it. Inside the ring of packed soil the decayed matter left from the post, and any organic packing material that was used, will usually be darker than the packed soil surrounding it.

These molds appear as small, round, dark spots when the soil above them is scraped away. When a circle like this appears, digging should stop and the location and size of the mold should be recorded. After that has been taken care of there are several methods of excavation that may be used. One is to dig around the mold from at least three sides, making sure that the mold is not disturbed by the digging, until the bottom of the mold is reached. Once you are sure that you have uncovered a post mold, and not a disturbance such as an animal burrow or the decayed remains of a large root, you begin searching the surrounding area for signs of other posts that may reveal a pattern of a building or fence line.

An alternate method is to assume the circle is a post mold, and attempt to find others in the surrounding area before excavating the first. If others are found, further excavation will depend upon the type of pattern found, and the construction habits of the people who inhabited the region being studied.

Post molds may be an indication of a large structure, a fence, or a ceremonial site, and are often accompanied by indications of walls and floors.

Buildings

Buildings, whether they are the remains of a hunting camp hut or a masonry wall mansion, offer a particular challenge for investigators. Almost all structures were built in a way that would disturb some of the strata at the building site, thereby possibly mixing artifacts from previous eras with those of the period when the building was constructed. In addition, many buildings were built with foundations, which required excavation and refilling, which further intermingled soil and other miscellaneous materials.

These factors, plus the problems of different strata on opposite sides of a wall at the same height, make it difficult to place artifacts in the correct sequence or strata. To overcome many of these problems the excavation of buildings is generally done in several phases. The first phase is to begin the digging a number of feet away from the structure. This is done for several reasons. One reason is to locate tools and utensils that may have been discarded as the building was constructed; another is to establish that the building either begins or ends where it appears to and to determine the highest level of the structure; and the last reason is to expose the profile of the surrounding strata. Several trenches may be dug at right angles to the walls of the building to help supply answers to these questions. These trenches are dug at least as far down as the bottom of the first strata outside the wall. Other trenches are then dug at right angles to the first ones to establish the location of the outside perimeter of the building.

After the outline of the building is located, the level of all the trenches is equal, and all information is duly recorded, the second phase of the excavation begins. This phase consists of proceeding downward, peeling away strata on both sides of the walls, until at least one full dwelling has been uncovered. The location of hearths, walls, post holes, floors, dumps, etc. are recorded, as well as the location of all artifacts. These records will provide clues to the nature of the occupation of the building.

Since the structure itself is a major interruption in the stratigraphy of the site, a special effort must be made to distinguish the record of the stratigraphy of the inside of the building from that of the outside. Even strata that appear to be on the same level may contain artifacts of different periods.

Mounds

Mounds are features common to many archaeological sites, particularly in the midwestern and southeastern portions of the United States. There are artificial mounds and natural mounds. While the interior of natural mounds consists of regular strata deposited by natural actions over a number of years, the interior of artificial mounds consists of a mixture of soil types brought to the mound by human activity from the surrounding area. This mixture shows none of the regular strata found in natural formations.

Natives of North America, as well as of other regions of the world, generally built mounds for four reasons. They were built as fortifications against invaders; as effigy mounds representing various animals; as artificial hills upon which buildings such as temples and residences for leaders were erected; and as burial sites. It is sometimes difficult to determine the use of a mound without conducting an excavation, but each of the uses is reflected by the particular nature of the artifacts found around a mound and these artifacts definitely identify a mound's purpose.

Archaeologists use one of four methods in excavating a mound. Two, *strip* and *sondage*, are seldom used today, but were popular in the past. The strip method involves removing parallel strips of soil from the mound. The sondage method involves digging a single, deep trench from the top of the mound to the bottom, a method similar to digging an initial test trench at an excavation.

The methods most commonly used today are the *quadrant* and *grid*. The quadrant method is to divide the mound into quarters, and then the opposing sections are excavated from the outer edge of the mound toward the center, with walls left so that a profile of the stratigraphy is available for study. This method allows a complete cross section of the mound to be excavated, while leaving the alternate cross sections undisturbed.

Most archaeologists prefer to use the normal grid method for excavating mounds, particularly larger ones, since it deals with smaller amounts of excavated area. This makes it easier to record strata, features, and found artifacts. Regardless of the method used to excavate a mound, all the ground rules of archaeological excavation, such as stratigraphy, recording, and mapping, apply as they do to the whole excavation.

Mound excavation normally continues stratum by stratum from the top of the mound to the bottom, with each stratum carefully recorded as it is excavated. Experienced and inexperienced excavators are always anxious to reach the lower strata as quickly as possible since the top ones represent the most recent occupations, and are, therefore, the least interesting. The uppermost strata must still be examined and recorded carefully, however, since artifacts may be located that add new information about how the occupants of those periods lived. Occasionally this new information will counter the prevailing theories about those cultures.

A director of an excavation may decide to stop the movement to the lower strata if an important building is discovered in a mound. In that case, the lower strata may be left undisturbed, and the building completely excavated.

Burials

Many pits, as well as mounds, include burials. The excavation of a human burial, while one of the most exciting events of an archaeological excavation, requires some of the most exacting techniques used in archaeology. Since the level of interest, and more importantly, the level of sophistication required of the excavator, rises tremendously when there is a discovery of a burial site, most of the work specific to this discovery is transferred to the more experienced personnel on the dig. You can still be helpful and involved during this process, if you remember some of the more important differences between burial excavations and normal operations.

Burial pits, and mounds, are often very similar in surface appearance to refuse deposits, thereby making them hard to recognize. One significant difference is that refuse pits are generally round, or almost so, and burial sites are a long oval. If you encounter such an oval, particularly if it has traces of red paint present, you should treat the find as a burial site until it is proven to be otherwise. Remains of a fire, or sharp stones or shells stuck into the surface of the pit or mound, are also indicators of a burial site.

When any of these indicators are present you should notify the field supervisor, then carefully clear all surface debris away. The outline of the burial hole must then be determined, and a trench

A team member uses a fine brush to gently remove debris from around a skeleton found in a burial site. Burial sites require some of the most delicate and precise work done in excavations. Photo courtesy of Earthwatch and taken by Robert Angell.

begun at least one foot from one side of the burial hole. This trench should be dug about two feet wide and four to six feet deep, or dug until the bottom of the trench is definitely below the bottom of the burial hole. This will leave the site on a raised platform when it is completely excavated.

During this whole process the back of the digger should never be to the burial site, and no one should walk or stand above the burial site. In addition, great care must be taken that no artifacts or skeleton pieces are dislodged from the burial hole.

The field supervisor or excavation director will probably take over the excavation at this stage, and carefully review all artifacts and human remains *in situ* as they are uncovered. A very detailed account of all remains and all artifacts is kept since each placement may be important in determining the religious activities, mortuary customs, and special physical traits of the people who conducted the burial. After documentation has been finished, the excavation of the burial site continues until it is completed, and the remains are removed for further study in the laboratory.

The features described above are the major features that archaeologists encounter during excavations. How they approach them during the excavation may well determine the validity of any theories they develop about the site after studying the finds.

Just as important to those theories, though, are the hundreds of smaller finds that are made at a normal excavation. In addition to large features, almost all excavations uncover many smaller artifacts that help tell the story of the people who left them behind.

Chapter 11

Artifacts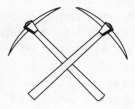

Large features, such as those discussed in the previous chapter, are always exciting to find, and doing so in conjunction with subsequent study adds immeasurably to the information we have about how previous societies lived. We more frequently unearth smaller artifacts, however, and it is from these that we gain most of our knowledge about the lives of the makers of the artifacts. Since decay is a natural process, and most archaeological excavations uncover sites that were occupied so long ago that most perishable materials have disintegrated, the vast majority of artifacts you will find at a site will be made of nonperishable material such as stone and fired clay.

In Chapter 9, I stated that objects unearthed during an excavation could fall into one of two categories—artifacts, which are human-made, and natural objects, which are not. I further noted that artifacts also fall into two categories—additive or subtractive.

Subtractive artifacts are common finds at prehistoric excavations, and the most common of these are *lithics*, or artifacts made of stone. Spear and arrow heads, blades of various types, and scraping tools were all made of stone by the earliest inhabitants of all continents.

To qualify as an artifact, a natural object must have been changed or modified by humans in some manner so it could

perform a specific function. Most of these objects were intentionally modified into a functional shape before they were used, but
others had shapes that were somewhat functional to early humans, and their shapes were gradually modified as they were
used. We can generally identify tools by obvious modifications
that were made in rocks or stones, but sometimes it is hard to
differentiate between changes brought about by natural processes
and those wrought by humans. Stone is polished, ground, and
fractured by water, ice, and wind, and many times the results of
these actions are indistinguishable from those resulting from in-
tentional modification.

Some artifacts, such as well-formed projectile points and axes,
are obvious to even the untrained observer. Earlier tools, which
were often only slightly modified fragments primarily formed by
natural actions, are more difficult to identify, however, and even
highly trained professionals sometimes violently disagree about
the authenticity of an artifact, or even a whole site.

One such site is Calico in the Mojave Desert of Southern California. There, a group of archaeologists claim to have found an
early site that contains stone chips and flakes which, they say,
proves that humans were in the region as long ago as 200,000 B.P.
This is in dramatic contrast to the more accepted claim that human
occupation in the region goes back only about 10,000 years. The
source of the dispute between the two groups is the determination
by the proponents of the earlier date that various stone chips and
flakes they have discovered are fragments cast aside by early
toolmakers. Their opponents claim the chips and flakes are the
results of natural processes, and that the objects show no indications of human modification.

With such disparate interpretations of objects by respected
professionals, it is easy to see how novice archaeologists could
miss an important artifact while sifting through soil that has been
removed at an excavation. It is important to be able to distinguish
between work done by humans and that done by nature because
an artifact made by humans reveals many things about the people
who made it. The skill level required to make the artifact, the
special techniques and designs that may have been incorporated,

and the type of material used to make it all provide clues to the maker of the artifact. In a real sense, an artifact is a true reflection of the level of sophistication of the maker, and the type of existence he or she lived.

Chipped Stone

Humans adapted stone to tools and weapons in several ways. One method was chipping. This process was used to make arrow and spear heads, knives, and many types of scraping and drilling tools from hard stones such as flint, chert, quartz, and basalt. All of these stones have conchoidal fractures, elevations or depressions that resemble the inside of clamshells. By using one of the methods described below, flakes could be removed and modified.

Chipping was done either by using *percussion*, where one stone was used to strike another, thereby chipping off flakes, or by *pressure flaking*, where a pointed tool such as an antler tip was used to detach a flake by applying pressure on a thin edge of a stone.

A majority of the artifacts you will find during an excavation will be those made from chipped stone. Your field supervisor or excavation director will give you instruction about the types of artifacts you will probably encounter during the excavation, and you will soon learn to identify not only complete artifacts, but also small portions of partially worked ones, as well as chips and flakes that were left as waste as artifacts were made.

In summary, chipped stone artifacts can be recognized by indications of a regular pattern of chipping that modified the shape of the article; a shape that is similar to artifacts already identified; a large number of similarly shaped objects found at one site; indications of repeated use such as a broken edge or highly polished surface. You, as a novice, won't be required to make final judgement on whether or not a found object is an artifact or natural occurrence, but it will help everyone involved in an excavation if you can make some preliminary judgements as you uncover fragments of stone material.

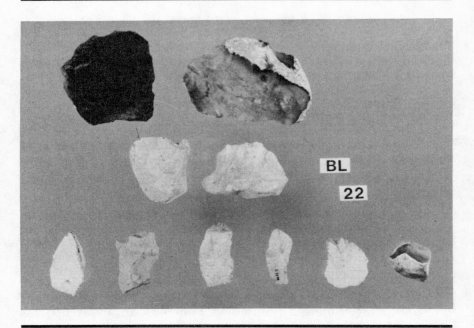

It is easy to see from looking at these chipped lithics how an investigator can overlook important artifacts among piles of naturally chipped and flaked stones during an excavation. Photo courtesy of Earthwatch.

Other Stone Artifacts

Stone was also modified by early humans using a technique that is generally described as *pecking, grinding, and polishing.* Mortars and pestles, gouges, and some axes were made by this method. Stone material with a rough, natural shape that closely resembled the envisioned finished product was beaten into a more finished shape by the use of a hammerstone, leaving evidence of the crushing or pecking action on the surface of the artifact. Sometimes certain portions of the artifact, such as a cutting edge or flat grinding surface, were polished smooth by the use of some abrasive substance.

It is often difficult to distinguish between chipping, grinding, and pecking done by humans, and that done by nature. Stones that have been pitted by the erosive action of rushing water and small pebbles may be confused with grinding mortars made by early humans. The flakes and chips under dispute at the Calico Site are an excellent example of the need for collaborating evidence when attempting to identify a find as modified by human or natural means.

Pottery

One indication of the early civilization of humans was the development of pottery. Pottery products are examples of additive artifacts, because the final products are significantly different in appearance from the material used to make them. Soon after humans learned to fire-harden clay, different cultures began to develop individual pottery-making styles and techniques that, to this day, help us establish a chronology of archaeological sites. These chronologies are determined largely by the types and styles of pottery artifacts found in various strata. The styles and techniques of different groups were so distinctive that sometimes a single sherd may help us identify the period a site represents.

Archaeologists recognize the important role pottery artifacts have in the recreation of the life of early humans, and they often give short courses in pottery to novice archaeologists participating on an excavation to help the novices more easily identify finds. One archaeologist, William Waldren, who conducts excavations on Spain's Balearic Islands, even goes so far as to have dig participants actually make pottery, using techniques similar to those used by the culture he is studying.

Other Artifacts

While stone and fire-hardened clay were the most common materials used to make the artifacts unearthed by today's

This volunteer is using a brush to carefully remove material from the outside of a fragile pot without destroying it. Photo courtesy of the Foundation for Field Research.

excavations, earlier societies used many other materials to make tools, utensils, and other objects. Artifacts made of bone, antlers, and shells are frequently found in more recent sites, or in sites where the conditions were conducive to the preservation of these more perishable materials.

Even more perishable materials such as skins, textiles woven from hair or vegetable fibers, and baskets made from various materials are seldom uncovered except in very arid regions around the world such as the southwestern deserts of North America. When artifacts of this kind are uncovered they provide a great deal of information about the cultures being studied.

When the historic period of a site is closer to the present, more and more artifacts made of durable materials such as copper and

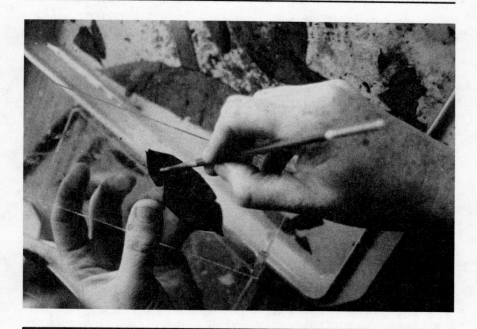

A 3000-year-old leaf is brushed clean with a small paint brush, and held steady with a piece of glass. Many objects uncovered in excavations are extremely fragile, and require tender, loving care if they are to be preserved. Photo courtesy of Earthwatch and taken by George Alsup.

iron are found, and these can easily be dated. This allows archaeologists to give a more precise date to the site, rather than a relative one based on surrounding strata.

Once again I want to point out that none of the artifacts uncovered, regardless of their quality or nature, are of much use to archaeologists, particularly those who may wish to study the results of an excavation later, unless information about the excavation, and the artifacts, is recorded in a systematic manner.

Chapter 12

Recording an Excavation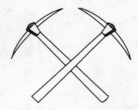

The need for full and concise documentation of all aspects of an excavation has been repeated throughout the first part of this book, and the processes involved in mapping the site and preparing the grid layout have been explained. The map and grid layout are completed before excavation begins on a site, and they are used by field supervisors as guides to help them accurately record information about artifacts and other features that are unearthed during the excavation. Most of the information about the excavation is recorded on standard forms, or common derivations thereof, that are designed to present details in as concise and clear a manner as is possible.

The key words here are *concise* and *clear*, because records that are filled with superfluous information and nebulous words are hard to interpret by investigators who did not work on the excavation. At every stage, all workers must strive to impart all the factual information about a find in as few words as possible, and in the simplest manner possible. This will make misinterpretations less likely when the information is transcribed from one document to another, and will make the final report true to the findings at the actual excavation.

Report Forms

A number of forms are standard to almost all excavations. Following is a brief description of each of the most common forms.

Site Report

This is the first form filled out about an excavation, and includes general information such as the name of the site, the type of excavation, the location, and the name of the owner of the land where the excavation is taking place.

Daily Field Report

This report describes each day's activities at the site, including the location of the day's excavations, who was involved, how long they worked, and what they found. General notes such as weather conditions, difficulties encountered during the day, and progress of the excavation are also included.

Feature Register

This report covers all artifacts and features uncovered during the day. After an artifact has been numbered, tagged, and placed in a safe container, a report is written that includes the artifact's assigned number, the grid coordinates where it was found, a full description of the artifact, and information about the stratigraphy where the artifact was located. Other information such as the nature of artifacts found nearby, unusual qualities of the artifact, and miscellaneous thoughts about the find are also noted on this report.

Stratigraphy Record

This report gives a precise statement of all the characteristics of every stratum uncovered during the excavation. This includes a description and the measurements of each. The description includes information about the type of soil (loam, sand, gravel) and

Site Number _____   Site Name _____

City_____   County _____   State _____

USGS Map Name and Coordinates _____

Directions for Reaching Site _____

_____

_____

Site Owner _____

Address of Site _____

Name of Tenant on Site _____

Attitude of Owner about Excavation _____

General Description of Site _____

_____

_____

Type of Site _____   Approx. Depth of Site _____

Size of Site _____   Vegetation on Site _____

Type of Soil on Site_____   Nearest Water to Site _____

Site Damaged or Inaccessible _____   How _____

Known Features of Site _____

Previous Excavations at Site _____

Additional Information on Site _____

_____

Site Reported To _____

Reported By _____

Additional Remarks _____

_____

Recorded By _____   Date _____

*Most report forms are general enough so they can be used at any site,
historical or prehistorical, and many archaeological societies and
organizations provide standard forms for members to use. This is an
Archaeological Site Report.*

Site Name and Number _____ Recorder _____

Date _____ Exc. Day # _____ Time Begun _____ Ended _____

Excavated By _____ Assisted By _____

Sections or Units Worked _____ Depth _____

Features Found or Worked _____

Description _____

_____

Comments and Observations on Features _____

_____

Artifacts Found (Be Specific in Description and Sketch Below) _____

_____

_____

_____

Comments and Observations on Artifacts _____

_____

Day's Weather Conditions _____

Interpretations of Day's Finds _____

_____

Special Difficulties of Day _____

_____

Daily Field Report.

Site Name and Number _____ Recorder _____

Date Found _____ Day Number _____ Time Found _____

Feature Name _____ Feature Number _____

Grid Coordinates Where Feature Found _____

Depth from Surface _____ Strata Number _____

Size of Feature _____ Shape _____

Description of Feature _____

_____

Discussion of Feature _____

_____

Other Objects Associated with Feature _____

_____

Artifact Name _____ Artifact Number _____

Grid Coordinates Where Artifact Found _____

Depth from Surface _____ Strata Number _____

Size of Artifact _____ Shape _____

Description of Artifact _____

_____

Discussion of Artifact _____

_____

Other Objects Associated with Artifact _____

_____

Disposition of Artifact _____

Sketch Features and Artifacts on Reverse Side

Feature Register.

North Bloomfield Chinatown Project: Surface Collection

Date _____   Unit _____

Recorded By _____   Unit Size _____

Ceramics

Bamboo _____   Four Flowers _____   Celadon _____

Double Hap. _____   Brown Glazed _____   Pipe Bowl _____

Other Asian _____

Euroamerican _____   TOTAL _____

Glass

Bottle _____   Window _____   Table _____

Chn. Vial _____   Lighting _____   Other _____

TOTAL _____

Metal

Cans _____   Wire Nail _____   Square Nail _____

Opium Tin _____   Other _____   TOTAL _____

Other

Game Counter _____   Button _____   TOTAL _____

Notes

Fire Affected _____   TOTAL NUMBER OF ARTIFACTS _____

Some investigators develop their own specialized forms for use at specific sites. The Surface Collection Report form from the North Bloomfield Chinatown Project is an example. The project director developed this form because the team was finding such large numbers of artifacts, primarily fragments, on the surface at the site.

its texture (fine, coarse, thick). The measurements include both the distance each stratum begins below the surface and its depth.

Photo and/or Sketch Report

This report accompanies any photos taken or sketches made during the day. It includes the date, the artifact number, the roll number of the film, the negative number on that roll, an explanation of film exposure and type of film used, the direction the camera is pointing, and any other identifying information about the photo that will help answer any questions about what the photo represents.

Scale sticks or other objects that suggest the scale of the object being photographed are a must in archaeological photography, and the photographer should have a variety of sizes handy to use in all settings. Sign boards that indicate the date, site, trench, stratum, and other clarifying information may also be used, although some archaeologists feel that these aren't necessary if sufficient written records are kept.

Burial Report

Burial reports are more complicated than normal artifact reports. For that reason they are done on a separate form, and include more information. In addition to the information normally included on an artifact report a burial report includes the position of the skeleton (extended, flexed, etc.), the compass orientation of the skeleton, the quality of preservation, and a description of body ornaments and personal belongings that are found with the skeleton.

Exact measurements, as well as sketches and photographs should also be included in the report.

Daily Field Journal

This journal includes information from all of the reports described above, and is usually written at the end of each day by the field supervisor or expedition director. Various comments made by team members are often included in the journal after the day's excavation has been discussed in the evening.

Notation System

While the need to be clear and concise in recording information on the forms has been stated, this is impossible without a notation system that is used by everyone on the excavation. Each expedition director devises a notation system which is used by all workers on that expedition to identify and record all strata, features and finds. The same system is used when the expedition's reports are written.

Level Tags

As each new stratum is identified, a tag or label should be stuck into the exposed wall to actually mark the level. The notations on the tag should include much of the information noted in the reports described above. The tag is a simplified notation of that information, and should include the site code number, the specific square or trench code number, and the stratum code number. A brief description of the stratum is often added beneath the code numbers.

These tags are placed at intervals along the walls of the trench, and can be attached with large staples, or other pointed objects, such as nails, that will not cause the wall to cave in.

Artifact Tags

All found artifacts must be tagged in much the same manner as the strata. Duplicates should be made of these tags, with one to be attached to the artifact, and the other to be attached to the outside of the container in which the artifact is placed. In addition to all of the information that was included on the level tag, artifact tags should also include the date the find was made, and the initials of the person who found it and of the site supervisor who checked it.

Most site supervisors store artifacts in individual paper bags or boxes so that materials removed from different strata or collected on different days aren't inadvertently mixed together.

After the information about the artifacts is recorded in the daily report of the excavation, and the artifacts are appropriately tagged, they are either stored so they can be studied in a laboratory at a later date, or taken to the lab site at the excavation for more immediate examination.

At the lab the artifacts are sorted, cleaned, preserved if needed, and readied for study.

Chapter 13

In the Laboratory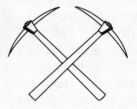

It has been estimated that for every hour of work in the field there are three spent in the laboratory. The work in the lab is classification and interpretation of the artifacts uncovered during the excavation. It is done in preparation for writing the site report because there are a number of questions that must be answered about each artifact before a site report can be written.

The archaeologist must identify the object, determine its use, estimate when it was made and how, and make some educated guesses about what happened to it from the time it was made until it was unearthed. In addition, the significance of the artifact to the understanding of the site, particularly the age of the artifact, must be resolved.

The first step in answering these questions, and one that is often done in the field, is the step of cleaning all the artifacts so they can be identified and sorted. Cleaning isn't always a simple matter, and shouldn't be attempted by anyone who is unfamiliar with the various materials that are likely to be found at a site. Old paint may be scraped off along with dirt, and fragile artifacts can be destroyed when cleaned with stiff brushes.

As artifacts are uncovered their environment changes, and degradation of material can occur quickly if the proper steps aren't taken in cleaning and preservation. Wood that has survived almost intact in water will rapidly decay if left out of water; iron that has only slightly rusted will oxidize much more quickly if washed in water; bone that was buried in wet soil will crack and split if left out in the sun to dry, and even stone will flake if surface salts aren't removed with soap and warm water.

All of the steps made to clean or preserve artifacts, whether done in the field or in the lab, must be carefully recorded so that future investigators can know what was done. Sometimes new techniques of preservation are developed, and those people working on the artifacts must know what was done previously. At other times, tests may be run that require knowledge of the chemicals that were used to clean the artifacts.

Materials present their own particular problems when they must be cleaned and preserved, and you will be given precise instructions by a supervisor if you are assigned to cleaning duties. No novice should ever attempt to clean artifacts without instruction and supervision, and the following information is only meant to introduce you to some of the procedures used in the lab.

Before either cleaning or preservation begins, the correct identification of the material being dealt with must be established. Too vigorous an action can completely destroy many fragile artifacts, and the use of wrong cleaning and preservation materials can destroy others, even those made of stone or iron.

After the material used to make the artifact is determined, steps, specific to the type of material being cleaned, may be taken.

Lithics

Unpainted stone objects can be cleaned in warm water and soap to remove any surface salts. If these aren't removed they will recrystallize, which can cause flaking. Painted stone should be cleaned carefully by a soft brush so that the paint will not be removed by the cleaning process.

Precious Metals

Gold and silver are both fragile, and are easily scratched by hard objects. Gold can be washed gently in warm water and soap, but silver should only be carefully brushed.

Bronze

Bronze should only be cleaned with a soft brush. If the object is dry, it should be stored in a dry place; if it is wet, it should be dried slowly in a controlled atmosphere before being stored.

Iron

If an iron object is badly rusted it can be cleaned in water and carbonate of soda, then thoroughly dried in an oven or by other quick means. If it is only slightly rusted, the rust is best removed with a hard brush, and the artifact should not be washed. In either case it should be stored in a dry place.

Wood

If wood is going to be analyzed, it must be kept in the same environment that it was found in, and immediately taken to the lab for study. If it is not going to be analyzed, it should, if found dry, be kept in a dry, enclosed place. If it was wet when it was found, it can be dried slowly, away from the sun, at about 60 degrees or it can be kept wet in a water and alcohol mixture until it is studied completely.

Pottery

Some hard-fired pottery can be washed, but to be on the safe side, it should be cleaned only with a soft brush.

Certification for Lab Technicians

All of the materials discussed above, plus many more that were not mentioned, are preserved using a variety of techniques that have been developed over the years. All preservation work must be done directly under the supervision of a trained expert. Some organizations, such as the field school at Colonial Williamsburg, offer classes in laboratory work, and award certification for lab technicians. Any of you who are particularly interested in pursuing this specialty should contact archaeological societies in your area to see if they offer such a program.

Further Steps Taken in the Lab

After artifacts have been cleaned, preserved, and sorted to type, numbers are applied to each that indicate site number, strata number, and feature number. These numbers are then used to help workers sort the artifacts into groups and subgroups. For sherds of pottery and ceramics, this may mean sorting and re-sorting until the sherds are grouped by individual pots or vessels. For other types of artifacts it may mean sorting all iron pieces together, or combining all surviving pieces of leather. At this point some artifacts may be mended so they can be displayed in a museum exhibit or preserved in archives.

One last step remains before the site report is written, and that is to date the artifacts.

Dating Techniques

There are two types of dating methods that archaeologists use. One is *relative dating*, which is based upon the stratigraphy of the site, and the other is *absolute dating*, which gives a specific date to an artifact or a site stratum. In the true sense of the word, relative dating isn't really dating. No specific or absolute time chronology is involved. An archaeologist can only determine how groups of artifacts, or strata at an excavation, relate to each other in a general time frame. With relative dating we can determine that artifacts in Group A are older than those in Group B, and those in Group B are older than those in Group C, but we cannot tell exactly when the artifacts were made or used.

The goal of all archaeologists is to go beyond relative dating, and establish an absolute chronology that defines not only the specific date, or set of dates, that an artifact was made or a site inhabited, but to attribute definite time periods to various sites.

Establishing relative chronology is easy (that is, if the site hasn't been turned topsy-turvy by activity subsequent to the deposition of the material being studied), but much more sophisticated techniques are needed to establish absolute dating.

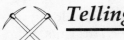

Telling Time Backwards

Earlier I mentioned that archaeologists often enlist the support of professionals outside their own field, and this collaboration is most evident when archaeologists are attempting to determine the ages of artifacts and sites. Some of the techniques used in dating objects are generally accepted by archaeologists, while others are more controversial. All, however, help answer one of the most frequently asked questions about archaeological artifacts, How old are those objects?

Geology

Geologists study the earth and the natural forces that are involved in changes that take place. One aspect of this study is the study of time. Geologists develop dates for various geological stages by relating them to climatic and geologic events that have been documented, but these are relative dates, not absolutes. Nevertheless, they do help archaeologists confirm some of their relative chronologies, and both fields use stratigraphy as the basis of these dating techniques.

It is possible for geologists to determine absolute dates for geological occurrences, but most of the methods they use are accurate only when they are dealing with millions of years, not for tens of thousands.

Dendrochronology

A sequential record of climatic changes is found in trees by examination of the concentric circles of wood. A new circle, or layer, is added each year. The rings that develop each season reflect favorable and unfavorable years of tree growth. When rains are plentiful, the rings are broad. When there is a dearth of moisture, the rings are narrow.

The study of these rings by an astronomer at the University of Arizona, who wished to document the effects of sunspot activities on weather, has led to the development of a master chart of tree rings that dates the rings back to approximately 7000 B.P. This chart can be used to match the tree rings visible in building materials from archaeological sites to rings on the chart, thus establishing absolute dates for the building. One important region where the use of this technique has provided excellent information is the southwestern United States, where archaeologists have been able to date the construction of Anasazi dwellings.

The rings in the timbers used as rafters in the pueblos were matched against the master chart to determine not only the dates the trees sprouted, but the dates the trees were cut and used in the buildings.

While dendrochronology is very useful in establishing absolute dates at archaeological sites it has several limitations. One limitation is that in regions such as the humid, eastern sections of the United States and Canada, very little wood survives long enough to enable archaeologists to construct any sort of master chart. Another is that the trees used by early builders may not have well-defined growth rings.

If the environment is conducive to the preservation of wood, and the outer rings of wood used in construction are present, dating can be done using a master chart, developed for the region, to determine the absolute age of a building.

Pollen Analysis

Pollen analysis is similar to dendrochronology in that it depends upon the interpretation of climatic records. This technique uses layers of pollen that have accumulated in wetlands where at least moderately accurate sequences of deposition dates have been established.

A sample of material taken from a stratum is studied, and then compared to samples of material with known sequences that have been taken from selected sites in the region. From the results, archaeologists can determine fairly accurate absolute dates for strata, and they can gain information about a society's interactions with the environment of the region being studied.

Pollen analysis has been used sparingly as a dating technique, because worldwide tables have yet to be developed. It has gained more popularity as a technique for determining how earlier people used plants, and establishing relative dates of when people began to develop cultivated plants.

Carbon 14

Geologists and paleontologists have long been able to measure the dates of fossils and rocks through the measurement of radioactive decay of various elements such as Uranium 238. The disintegration of most of these elements is so slow that, as a definable period of time, it is not a useful yardstick for archaeologists, who deal in tens of thousands of years instead of millions and tens of millions of years.

In 1931, scientists at the University of Chicago discovered carbon 14, a previously unknown source of radioactivity. This element had a half-life of just over 5500 years, which made it a more useful tool for archaeologists, and archaeologists now use it to help date artifacts up to about 40,000 B.P.

All living organisms either ingest or inhale carbon 14 while they are alive, and the element begins to disintegrate as soon as the organism dies.

Researchers can test artifacts that are the remains of previously living organisms for carbon 14, and determine fairly reliable absolute dates for their deaths.

All of the above techniques used to determine both relative and absolute ages of found artifacts depend upon many variables, and require trained experts to apply them. Your involvement in the actual dating process will be minimal, if there is any involvement at all.

The purpose of the procedures discussed in this chapter is to study artifacts that were systematically excavated in preparation for the final stage of all excavations—the writing of the site report. Although archaeology has been described as a scientific discipline, all the work done on an excavation is meaningless unless the results of that work are shared with others in the field. This sharing is done through a publication of results of the excavation. This site report may be a short article published in the newsletter of a local archaeological society; a longer article published in a respected state, national, or international archaeology journal; or a full-length book.

Regardless of where the results are published, they should present, in a clear and concise manner, a report of the excavated site that describes the methods used, as well as an interpretation of all finds made during the excavation and the results of all of the follow-up studies.

While site reports are often thought of as the responsibility of professionals, many are written by advanced amateurs, and are fully accepted by professionals in the field.

Chapter 14

Writing the Final Site Report

Because the purpose of an excavation is to further our knowledge about the early inhabitants of a region, it is necessary to make a report of all of the evidence discovered during a dig and of the analysis made of these finds. While the extensive reports and notes kept during the excavation may be useful in refreshing the memory of the people who actually worked on the dig, the data included in the reports will slowly become unintelligible, even to them, as time passes. The information is of even less use for investigators who did not work on the site. A final report, therefore, is necessary if the excavation is to fulfil its purpose of furthering knowledge about the site under investigation.

It is important that a final report be written while the information is fresh in everyone's mind, and amateur participants on the excavation, especially those with good writing skills, may become involved with the process, although this task is normally the responsibility of the professionals and advanced amateurs who organized the project.

A general pattern for the report is followed by most archaeologists—a pattern that incorporates an *abstract* (a short statement of the purpose of the paper, procedures used during the excavation, artifacts discovered, and conclusions made based on the information gathered), a presentation of the factual evidence uncovered during the excavation, and conclusions drawn by the principal investigators; all of these to be supported by inclusion of tables and illustrations. While the conclusions drawn by the investigators are always subject to controversy and disagreement, the factual presentation should not be. If an excavation has been correctly administered, and proper procedures have been followed in recording information about the excavation, anyone should be able to reconstruct, at least theoretically, the site and agree with the evidence presented.

Clear and *concise* were key words when the daily reports were discussed earlier, and they are just as important when discussing final reports. Readers of the report must understand what the people involved with the excavation hoped to find, what was found, where it was found, the techniques used during the excavation, and how the finds were interpreted. A typical final report will include the elements described below.

Introduction

The report should begin with an introduction, which should include information about how a site was selected, why it was selected, and who worked on it.

Site Description

Details about the site are included in this section of the report. The geographical location of the site, with references to state, city, county, and other political divisions, is given, and all permanent markers near the site, such as benchmarks or survey posts, should be mentioned. Directions to the site, with specific distances along named or numbered roads and highways, are given so anyone can locate it easily.

Any history that is relevant to the excavation can be given in this section.

After the geographical location and history of the site is given, a description of the particular topography of the site is furnished in detail. Whether the land was wooded, open, or cultivated is indicated, and natural features, such as hills, creeks, lakes, marsh, and large boulders or rock piles, are mentioned.

Finally, the location of the baseline marker should be accurately described, and distances and bearings from some large natural feature that is unlikely to be disturbed in the foreseeable future should be cited.

Methodology

This section should give complete descriptions of the excavation methods used, the way records were kept, and the forms used to record information. This section is most important for future investigators, and is the best indicator in the report of the reliability of the facts presented and conclusions drawn about the excavation.

Excavation Finds

This section presents evidence and facts about any artifacts and features uncovered during the excavation, and any data that was gathered during the analysis stage of the excavation. It is important that conclusions about the site are kept out of this section, because an unbiased presentation of the discoveries made at the site is required in a final report. Conclusions come later.

A description of the stratigraphy of the site is the first information presented in this section. Any disturbances unearthed should be reported, and shown on the grid map which is included in the report.

The stratigraphy report should be followed by a report on all features such as hearths, pits, and walls. Illustrations of typical features, as well as specific illustrations of any unusual ones, should accompany this section. If a burial was found during the excavation all the information relating to it should be reported with great care, and an outside expert is generally used as a reference when preparing this part of the final report.

A description of the artifacts uncovered during the excavation is one of the most important aspects of this section. A clear description of all objects, as well as their precise vertical and horizontal locations in the excavation, is necessary for readers so that they may accurately compare them to other finds. Artifacts are generally divided into categories such as *lithics, pottery, bone, wood,* and *textiles,* and then into subgroups, such as chipped and polished artifacts, if there are sufficient numbers of these objects to justify doing this.

Literature Search

After the data about the excavation have been presented, the report should present data gathered from previously published literature about comparable sites both near to and distant from the report site. Opinions are often stated in this section, especially when there is some evidence of a connection, such as trade or migration, between sites. These assumptions are certainly open to question, however, so there should be a clear distinction between opinions and facts presented in the report.

Conclusion

After all of the evidence has been presented, conclusions can be drawn about the discoveries made at the excavation site. While it is hoped that all the conclusions are well-founded, and based on the evidence gathered during the excavation, they are open to debate. Such debate is an integral part of science, though, and should be expected.

Where Do You Go from Here?

When the final report is finished an excavation is complete. This, however, is usually just the beginning for amateur archaeologists, because most people can't dig only once. The dust and dirt gets into the skin and the desire to quest for answers lodges in the brain, and the memories of both sensations provoke the novice archaeologist to return to the field for yet another expedition. Soon the novice becomes a journeyman, then an advanced amateur, and, occasionally, a professional.

It is difficult to transmit the excitement and lure of an excavation through words alone. There is no substitute for observing an excavation on site where archaeologists can be observed, methodically peeling away layers of earth in search of a small artifact that tells a story of early humans, just as there is no substitute for actually getting down on your hands and knees in the dirt and dust and searching for treasures yourself.

Part Four of this book is a directory of organizations that will assist you in finding archaeological exhibits where you can view artifacts, tours to archaeological sites around the world, excavation sites where you can observe archaeologists at work, field schools where you can learn as you work, and excavations where you can join the crew to help unearth a site.

First, however, I have added Part Three, which is for those of you who can't wait to get out in the field, or have stumbled across what you think is an unknown archaeological site. In this section I have included some basic information about laws governing excavations, and given more details about how to conduct an extensive site survey, because conservation archaeology depends upon an informed citizenry that is willing to help define and protect our archaeological heritage.

Part Three

Working on Your Own

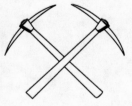

Chapter 15

The Lure of the Excavation

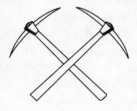

I devoted the first part of this book to encouraging readers to join ongoing excavations directed by experienced archaeologists, and I discouraged people from operating unsupervised digs. However, the thrill of discovering an ancient archaeological site and uncovering artifacts that reflect the lives of early humans can overwhelm even the most conservation-minded novice. When a new, undocumented site is located, lust may take precedence over prudence. When this happens, both the site and the archaeologist will suffer. The site may be damaged by amateur activities, and the archaeologist risks severe penalties for breaking the rules and regulations.

Because there is such a shortage of qualified archaeologists and personnel for supervising the excavation of documented sites around the world, there is a way to satisfy the lust while maintaining the integrity of the site and conservation archaeology.

Conservation archaeologists try to identify and map archaeological sites exactly as they find them, and then determine if there is just cause for invading, or excavating, the site. Salvage archaeologists attempt to rescue as much information and material as possible from a site that is in danger of being destroyed. Novices are welcomed by both of these groups, and may, eventually, work on excavations or conduct surveys that otherwise would never have been undertaken. Amateur archaeologists who crave an opportunity to participate in a dig can always find one, and it may even be near their homes.

As this book was being completed, two archaeological finds on the eastern coast of the United States surfaced, and the way they were handled by the amateur archaeologists who discovered them illustrates both the good and bad that can occur when ancient sites are discovered.

As Dan Carns, an amateur archaeologist, was walking along a Cape Cod beach in Fall 1990 he spotted a stone-lined fire pit that had been exposed along the face of a sand dune by high tides. Instead of attempting an excavation on his own, Carns reported his find to the local archaeological society, who, in turn, contacted archaeologists who were interested in the ancestors of the natives who met the Pilgrims when they landed in what is now Massachusetts.

The one-and-a-half-acre site of what may be the oldest structure in the Northeast was far from safe, even though local archaeologists were soon investigating it. Within a month or so after it was discovered the highest tides of the past 75 years inundated the site, and destroyed important evidence of early life on the Cape.

A salvage expedition was launched that unearthed tools, pottery, post molds, hearths, and pits; all similar to those uncovered in other sites that range from Newfoundland to South Carolina.

Because Dan Carns knew the importance of systematic excavations, an important archaeological site was, if not saved, at least salvaged. The same was not true of a similar site near Baltimore. At least not completely.

What may be the most important Early Archaic site ever discovered in Maryland became the cause of a race between a team of archaeologists, who were attempting to excavate the remarkable 8,000- to 10,000-year-old campsite and a single pot hunter, who destroyed dozens of features in a search for artifacts. The archaeologists who headed the salvage team stated that the damage done by the pot hunter was the worst they had ever encountered.

Even with the looting, the site remains one of the best Early Archaic sites in the region, and the team of salvage archaeologists found many features that tell about the life and behavior of the early inhabitants.

Both of these battles, one fought with nature and the other with a pot hunter, were publicized nationally by the media, and both resulted in good, but less than desirable, results. Even less than desirable results, however, are better than no results, which would have been the case in both instances if there had been no recognition of the importance of the archaeological sites by interested amateurs.

At both sites, the brunt of the salvage work fell on teams of amateurs who were directed by professional archaeologists, amateurs who were able to satisfy their desire for excavation on worthwhile projects.

There are some cases when amateurs can conduct a site survey or excavation, or, indeed, must do so if any knowledge is to be gained from an archaeological site. These are rare, however, and should only be undertaken by novices if no other options are available. If you find yourself in a position where you *must* conduct a site survey in order to preserve at least some knowledge of what is contained in the site, you should be extremely aware of the legal, as well as ethical, constraints that govern the investigation of archaeological sites.

Chapter 16

Following Laws and Regulations

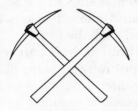

There have been laws and regulations governing the destruction or collection of antiquities since 1906 in the United States. That year, the first federal legislation was enacted. The Antiquities Act of 1906 recognized the need for government involvement with the protection of archaeological sites, or at least those on federal lands, and made unauthorized excavation of such sites a crime.

While this act was poorly enforced for a number of years, it did set a precedent for the funding of archaeologic research, and established the need for permits for excavations on federal lands. Today only qualified individuals may be given permits to excavate on those lands, and they must agree to deposit the results of all research with a public museum. Most permits for archaeological research are controlled by the National Park Service.

The authorization for this responsibility came from the Historic Sites Act of 1935, which said that archaeological and historic sites belong to the people, and that all efforts to preserve them be done for the public good. The National Park Service was specifically designated the responsibility for supervising research in this area. This act was more specific than the 1906 act about the need for active research, and declared it a national policy to fund and otherwise support archaeologic research.

A more specific statement about the recovery of archaeological materials on federal lands was made in the Reservoir Salvage Act of 1960. This act declared that federal construction projects, such as dams, must be halted if there is evidence that archaeological sites are threatened, and an attempt should be made to salvage the data contained in the sites before construction can resume. Since 1960, many states have modeled statutes implementing salvage archaeology processes after the Reservoir Salvage Act.

In 1966 the most important legislation ever enacted in the United States concerning historic and prehistoric preservation was passed. The Historic Preservation Act allowed the Historic Register to include many less than outstanding, but important, historic sites around the nation, and it established grants-in-aid to state agencies to help them designate sites. Many local and state statutes governing historic and prehistoric sites have been enacted as a result of this legislation, and numerous archaeological sites have been preserved because of these local ordinances.

Other pieces of federal legislation have followed, the National Environmental Policy Act of 1969, the National Historic Preservation Act of 1974, the Federal Land Policy and Management Act of 1976, and the Archaeological Resources Protection Act of 1979. All of these Acts directed federal agencies to establish a policy regarding the protection of historic and prehistoric sites, and have resulted in the preservation of archaeological sites that otherwise might have been plowed under and paved over.

One outgrowth of all of this legislation was the establishment of the federal Interagency Archaeological Salvage Program, which was formed to counsel federal agencies participating in dam construction about archaeological sites. The National Park Service was designated the coordinating agency for this program based on the Antiquities Act of 1906 and the Historic Sites Act of 1935, both of which gave the park service responsibility for supervising federal programs in this area.

For a number of years the enforcement of all federal acts was minimal, and state and local governments were slow to become involved. Today, however, almost all states have enacted fairly stringent legislation governing historic and prehistoric sites, and enforcement has increased significantly.

There is considerable variation in these laws and regulations from state to state, and you must determine what laws affect your activities if you begin a site survey, or anticipate forming an excavation team.

Alabama, for example, has a regulation that you must be a resident of the state to participate in an excavation there. Some states require permits for any excavation, including those done on private lands. Other states are more lax, and allow excavations to take place with minimum supervision even on state lands.

Throughout the United States and Canada, local, state and provincial archaeological societies join together with state, federal and provincial archaeologists to help disseminate information to aspiring archaeologists about all pertinent regulations, and the process amateurs and professionals must follow to obtain permission to excavate.

The Montana Archaeological Association, for example, publishes annually the *Professional Services Directory and Specialized Technical Resources Listing* that includes information about permit procedures.

The publication states that a state antiquity permit or land-use license is required for any survey, testing, or excavation conducted on state lands, and that these are issued by the Department of State Lands Archaeologist, who also makes compliance checks and reviews reports.

It also lists the federal agencies located in the state that issue permits for archaeological surveys and excavations, and tells what they require of permit applicants.

Notice that nothing has been mentioned about surveys and excavations on private lands. Montana, and many other states, have few rules and regulations governing archaeological sites on private lands.

That doesn't mean that you have either the ethical or legal right to simply enter private land and begin an archaeological survey. Private landowners retain the right to limit access to their property, and you must accept that right. In addition, you have certain ethical obligations to any landowner from whom you request the right to trespass.

Chapter 17

Beginning an Archaeological Survey

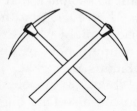

In its simplest form—and this is the type of survey you are most likely to be involved with—an archaeological survey is one or more people walking around an area attempting to find surface artifacts that indicate the presence of earlier human habitation. If any artifacts are sighted, their location is marked on the site survey map, and noted in the survey report. These artifacts may be historical or prehistorical in origin, and may be complete or fragmented, but they should be left in place when they are located. The only invasive activity that should occur during this time is the physical presence of the investigators on public or private property.

As noted above, some states such as Montana even require permits for surface surveys on public lands, and you should always contact landowners and tenants before encroaching on private lands. The latter is so important that the office of the Iowa State Archaeologist includes it as one requirement of basic skills and knowledge for individuals who wish to be certified as a site surveyor in the state.

When you suspect that there is an archaeological site on private property you should visit the landowner and/or tenant to explain that you would like to survey the property for evidence of an archaeological site. During this visit you can explain that a survey does not mean that an excavation will occur, but that you only want to establish that a site is indeed there. You should emphasize, however, that there is a possibility the local archaeological society might want to excavate later if the site shows promise of containing new or unusual evidence concerning the earlier inhabitants.

While you are obtaining permission to conduct a site survey you can also take the opportunity to question the owner/tenant about any information that may have been passed down as local lore about the region. This often leads to good clues about the location of sites, and give leads to the types of artifacts that may have been found there in the past.

Before you begin your site survey you should have the following basic skills:

- Be able to recognize the difference between types of sites such as mounds, campsites, villages, and so on.
- Be able to interpret topographical maps, and understand how to locate a site by quadrant, or quarter section.
- Be able to read a simple compass.
- Know what to collect from the site (fragments are just as important as complete artifacts in many cases, and nothing should be removed from its location unless it is likely to be disturbed or lost before an excavation takes place).
- Know how to properly describe all artifacts and features observed.
- Know how to complete a site survey form and draw a site map.

With these skills you will be able to adequately document a site, and report it to the local archaeological society or your state or provincial archaeologist for further action. The skills do not prepare you for conducting an excavation. If you persist in doing so you will be little better than the pot hunter who almost destroyed the site in Maryland.

There is one other skill that I didn't mention, and it is a skill that is extremely helpful to have available when conducting site surveys and developing the final site grid map. This is the ability to use survey techniques and tools such as transits. If you already have surveying skills you are a step ahead of most other amateur archaeologists. If you don't, you may want to consider investigating your local community college extension program to see if they offer any sort of survey courses. A basic course should be sufficient for your needs, and would make you a very desirable volunteer for almost every archaeological expedition.

There is a vast difference between reading about how something is done, and going out and doing it. Now that you have read this book you should be ready to go out and do something. Find an excavation nearby, or contact your local archaeological society and help with a site survey, or go on one of the archeological tours listed in the next section. Do any or all of these, but get involved, and help save our human heritage from useless destruction, whether that destruction is done by acts of commission or omission.

Part Four

Archaeological Resources

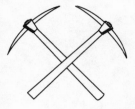

Chapter 18

The What's, Where's, and How-To's of Archaeological Activities

This section is a comprehensive resource to a wide variety of archaeological activities. These include travel agencies that offer guided tours of archaeological sites around the world; museums, primarily in the United States and Canada, that have extensive archaeological exhibits; archaeological sites in the United States, Canada, and other countries where visitors can observe work that has been done on excavations, and, in some cases, work currently underway; field schools where novices can learn the rudiments of excavation techniques; nonprofit archaeological organizations with open membership; organizations that act as clearinghouses for archaeologists who are looking for volunteer help on excavations; and ongoing excavations where novices can volunteer. A bibliography of books and periodicals that may be of interest to readers is also included in this section.

With this resource guide, and the information presented in the first three sections of this book, you should have no trouble locating archaeological activities that will satisfy your curiosity about the field, and you can join with other professionals and amateurs in pursuing knowledge of how earlier societies lived, survived, and flourished.

If no phone number is given a preference for contact by writing is requested.

Before You Leave

Before you begin your ventures into the world of archaeology there are some things you should consider. If you are going to visit museums or join an archaeological tour there should be few problems other than those normally encountered during travels away from home. If, however, you are planning to work on an excavation or attend a field school, there are a number of items to attend to before you leave home.

Read about where you are going. This will help you define your expectations more clearly, and add to the enjoyment of your trip. If you know about local customs before you reach an excavation, whether they are those of Native Americans of the southwestern United States or Bedouins of the Middle East, your experience is likely to be more exciting and fulfilling.

Make advance contact with the leaders of the excavation team to insure that you are welcome on the excavation, and will know what will be expected of you after you arrive. *Never* appear at a site unannounced and expect to be allowed to participate on an excavation. While this may be possible under very special conditions, it is never encouraged, and is considered rude and irresponsible by professional archaeologists. It is also illegal, in some countries, for a foreigner to work on an excavation without prior approval of a governmental agency that controls antiquities.

After you have made contact with an expedition, obtain information about the type of clothes that are most appropriate for working and leisure time (residents of some countries express strong disapproval of dress such as shorts and brief tops for example); the type of equipment you need to bring, if any; the amount of free time you will have for sight-seeing, and what the general schedule of the excavation team entails.

As you pack, keep in mind that you will probably have to carry your own luggage over considerable distances at various times during the trip. Some people suggest that you should never pack more than you can comfortably carry for a quarter-mile trot. This rule also insures that your luggage will not take up more of the limited space available on expedition vehicles than absolutely necessary.

Since many excavations are located in isolated regions and medical and dental care is often unavailable nearby, you should check about vaccinations that may be required in the region you are heading for (most expedition personnel suggest that anyone participating in an excavation have, at least, updated tetanus shots), and have health and dental examinations before you leave. You should also ask about health and dental insurance coverage. Some expeditions provide health insurance, while others require that you have your own.

Finally, make a checklist of small items that will make your trip more comfortable. These might include a small medicine kit with disinfectant and bandages; sunscreen, sunglasses, and hat; a small alarm clock; a good flashlight with extra batteries; reading material, including local guide books; pens, pencils, and notebooks; a canteen; and a good pocket knife. You may have additional items you would want to include, and the expedition director may suggest others.

Once you get to a site you become an important member of a team, and the effectiveness of that team depends upon its members being responsible. You can do your part by being familiar with the site being investigated, and what you will be expected to do there. Some of this information will come from material sent to you by the expedition director; other will come from your own reading about local customs and climate.

You can learn a lot during an excavation by watching others, and asking questions about what is going on. Many excavation leaders give informal instruction to volunteers during off hours. Sometimes this will cover the different skills required on the expedition, and other times it may include instruction about the site and what the director expects to find there.

Archaeological fieldwork isn't filled with the romance depicted in Hollywood productions. It usually takes place under less than ideal circumstances and in climates that are enervating. Nevertheless, disciplined attention to procedure and detail is demanded of all participants.

While working on a demanding project in a strange location even the best intentioned novice has moments of doubt about participating on a dig during "down" times. It is wise to set up a personal schedule during off hours that will help you maintain your equilibrium. Take time to clean your clothes, talk to others about how you feel, and keep a journal. A description of the work you are doing, and how you feel about the discoveries, or lack of them, the weather, evenings around the camp fire, and other daily occurrences will help you recount the excitement of your first expedition years later.

Travel Agencies

Below is a select list of travel agencies that specialize in tours to archaeological sites around the world. Some of these are very specialized, and lead tours to only one or two sites, thereby having extensive authority and knowledge about their subject. Others lead tours to a great number of sites that may vary from Egypt to Meso-America. While the latter may not have the intensive firsthand knowledge of the sites toured, they generally have local or university experts who lead groups.

I have listed special regions for some of the agencies, even though they may lead tours to other regions. Generally this is because they offer tours to regions that few others do.

For those who want to learn more about archaeology, but want to do so under more normal living circumstances than are offered at most excavations, tours are an excellent way to become involved in the subject. After this kind of introduction, some of you may progress to a field school or other participation in archaeology that involves more than observation.

Many travel agencies not specializing in archaeological tours can help you find trips that will meet your needs, but those that are listed below offer a wider variety of travel opportunities that involve archaeology.

Adventures in Anthropology
11740 San Vicente Blvd., #207
Los Angeles, CA 90049
213–626–7676

This organization offers a variety of Old and New World tours.

Aegean School of Classical Studies and Philosophy
946 "A" St.
Arcata, CA 95521
707–822–9668

This school offers a 35-day travel/study program of most major excavation sites throughout Greece.

American Studies Program
Anthropology Department/P 203B
Washington, DC 20052
202–994–6073

The Archaeological Conservancy
415 Orchard Dr.
Santa Fe, NM 87501
505–982–3278

This group leads tours of Southwest United States' archaeological sites, and acquires archaeological sites for preservation.

Archaeology Musica
PO Box 92
Cambridge, England
Tel. 011–44223–351069

This group has interactive tours that focus on music and musical instruments from before A.D. 1000.

Archaeological Tours
30 East 42nd St., Suite 1202A
New York, NY 10017
212–986–3054

Tours to Old World, New World, and Asian sites are offered by this agency.

Caiman Expeditions
3449 E. River Rd.
Tucson, AZ 85718
602–299–1047
800–365–ADVE

Tours to remote Mayan ruins of Meso-America are the focus of Caiman Expeditions.

Caravanas Voyages
1155–H Larry Mahan St.
El Paso, TX 79925
800–351–1685
In Canada: 800–63–RV–USA

Recreational vehicle (RV) caravans to archaeological sites of Mexico and Central America are coordinated by this group.

Cedok
10 East 40th St.
New York, NY 10016
212–689–9720

Cedok is the official Czech Travel Bureau and offers tours of the full archeological circuit in Czechoslovakia.

China Advocates
1635 Irving St.
San Francisco, CA 94122
415–665–4505
800–333–6474

This is a program offered in conjunction with the archaeology department of Peking University.

Club Voyages
PO Box 7648, Dept. A
Shrewsbury, NJ 07702
201–842–4946

Tours of archaeological sites of Turkey are a specialty of Club Voyages.

Colorado Institute
PO Box 875
Crested Butte, CO 81224
303–349–5118

Discover the world of ancient Indian cultures of Southwestern United States with this agency.

Columbus Travel
6017 Callaghan Rd.
San Antonio, TX 78228
800–225–2829

Tours of archaeological sites in Texas and Mexico can be arranged through this agency.

Cross Cultural Adventures
PO Box 3285
Arlington, VA 22203
703–243–7194
Telex 440283 ACI UI

Over the centuries the Berbers, Phoenicians, Greeks, Carthaginians, Romans, Vandals, Byzantines, Arabs, and French all came and made their home in Tunisia, the northernmost African land, and this agency specializes in tours to this region.

Crow Canyon Center for Southwestern Archaeology
23390 Country Road K
Cortez, CO 81321
303–565–8975

This is a permanent archaeological research and teaching facility at an Anasazi pueblo site in southwestern Colorado. Visitors are welcome, and amateur archaeologists may work on the excavation by arrangement. They also lead tours of other Anasazi sites in the Southwest.

Cultural Folk Tours International
10292 Gumbark Pl.
San Diego, CA 92131
619–566–5951
Outside California: 800–448–0515

Cultural tours, including museums and archaeology sites, of Turkey, Hungary, and Yugoslavia are conducted by this organization.

Discovery Tours
American Museum of Natural History
Central Park West at 79th St.
New York, NY 10024–5192
212–769–5700
800–462–8687

The Museum's program offers a wide variety of tours to all seven continents.

Exca-Vacations
PO Box 4261
Rapid City, SD 57709
605–342–1357

Exca-Vacations specializes in tours to current excavations.

Far Horizons
PO Box 1529
16 Fern Lane
San Anselmo, CA 94960
415–457–4575
Fax 415–457–4608

Tours in both the New World and the Old World can be arranged through this agency.

Forum Travel International
2437 Durant Ave., #208
Berkeley, CA 94704
415–843–8294

This agency leads tours to the Inca ruins of Peru and Bolivia.

FreeGate Tourism, Inc.
1156 Avenue of the Americas, #720
New York, NY 10036
212–764–1818
800–223–0304

Tours of classical sites in Greece, Italy, and Turkey are organized by this organization.

GEO Expeditions
PO Box 27136–STB
Oakland, CA 94602
415–530–4146

The rich, Inca ruins of Peru are the focus of tours led by GEO.

Globe Tours, Inc.
369 East Clearview
Worthington, OH 43085
614–846–4598

This is another agency offering classical tours of Greece, Italy, Turkey, and Egypt.

Great Journeys
Jameson Travel, Inc.
PO Box 669
Ipswich, MA 01938
508–356–1272
Outside Massachusetts: 800–225–2553

Tours around the world are led by historians and other lecturers.

Hanns Ebensten Travel, Inc.
513 Fleming St.
Key West, FL 33040
305–294–8174

Tours of sites and museums in Egypt are a specific focus of this organization.

Helios Travel
410 North Broad St.
Elizabeth, NJ 07208
201–353–6450
Fax 201–354–4575

Tours to archaeological sites and museums of ancient Egypt are arranged by this travel agency.

International Expeditions, Inc.
1776 Independence Court, Suite 104
Birmingham, AL 35216
205–870–5550

Tours to archaeological sites in the New World are coordinated by International Expeditions.

International Travel Program
15 East 84th St.
New York, NY 10028
212–879–4588
Fax 219–249–3672

International Travel Program offers a number of tours to archaeological sites around the world.

Journey to the East, Inc.
PO Box 1334
Flushing, NY 11352–1334
718–358–4034

This is an agency offering tours to museums and archaeological sites in China.

Journeys Unlimited
PO Box 16257
Santa Fe, NM 87506
505–989–9501
800–333–7574

Journeys Unlimited leads tours to Central and South America and has led archaeological tours for women only.

Ki Tours
PO Box 1566
Durham, NC 27704
800–767–8252

Ki leads tours to ancient, sacred sites around the world.

Lindblad Travel, Inc.
PO Box 912
Westport, CT 06881
203–226–8531
Telex 221412

The Kharga and Dakhla oases lie approximately one hundred and fifty miles southwest of Assiut and eighty miles due west of the Valley of the Kings in Egypt, and that is one site tour arranged by Lindblad. This agency offers a wide variety of archaeological tours, many in conjunction with museums.

Mayan Adventure Tours
PO Box 15204
Seattle, WA 98115
206–523–5309

Museum and archaeological tours of Mayan ruins in Yucatan, Belize, and Guatemala are the focus of this specialized travel group.

Mexi-Mayan Academic Travel
2216 W. 112th St.
Chicago, IL 60643
312–233–1711
Fax 312–239–1208

Mexi-Mayan Academic Travel offers archaeological tours of Mexico and Central America.

Nature Expeditions International
474 Williamette Ave.
PO Box 11496
Eugene, OR 97440
503–484–6529

On special cultural expeditions, you'll experience the incredible variety in Mexico and visit archaeological sites and museums.

Newfoundland Nature Tours
PO Box 1734
St. John's, NF A1C 5P5
709–576–6820
Fax 709–576–0208

This agency offers small, customized tours to archaeological sites in Newfoundland.

New Zealand Adventures
11701 Meridian Ave., North
Seattle, WA 98133
206–364–0160

Some of the tours arranged by this agency explore Maori archaeological sites.

Plantagenet Tours
85 The Grove
Moordown
Bournemouth BH9 2TY, England
800–521–4556

Tours of Middle Age European sites and museums are a specialty of this British company.

Regal Tours, Ltd.
1029 Teaneck Rd.
Teaneck, NJ 07666
201–837–8717

The tours are conducted in association with various museums and sites are generally selected to match the museums' permanent exhibits.

Serenissima Travel, Ltd.
2 Lower Sloane St.
London SWIW 8BJ, England
Tel. 01–730–7281

Crete is a specialty of the archeological tours offered here, and the many sites visited were homes of the great and mysterious Minoan civilization.

Smithsonian Associates Travel Program
Smithsonian Institution
Washington, DC 20560
202–357–4700

The Smithsonian Institution offers both domestic and foreign study tours, many of which feature archaeology.

Society Expeditions
3131 Elliott Ave., Suite 700
Seattle, WA 98121
206–285–9400
Fax 206–285–7917

Society Expeditions specializes in New World sites.

Unitrez
1043 E. Green St.
Pasadena, CA 91106
800–421–5744

None of the early explorers visited as many sites as you will on Mexican archeological adventures led by this agency.

Viking Tours of Greece
6 Turkey Hill Road South
Westport, CT 06880
203–226–7911
800–341–3030

The tours to these classical sites are led by professors.

Museums

Museums have always played an important role in archaeology, from sponsoring excavations to providing a place where archaeological collections can be stored, studied, and exhibited. They provide a wide variety of opportunities for amateur archaeologists. There are exhibits to be studied, archaeological tours led by museum staff to be enjoyed, volunteer positions such as guards, lab assistants, and docents to be filled, and museum-sponsored excavations to be joined. Not all museums offer all these opportunities, but most offer more than one.

The museums listed below are only a small portion of those around the world that house archaeological collections, but they are a good cross section of what is available. They range from large museums, such as the Field Museum of Natural History in Chicago where huge archaeological collections from worldwide sites are stored, to regional museums sponsored by small-town historical societies that house limited collections representative of the region.

All, however, can add to your enjoyment and understanding of archaeology, and you should never miss an opportunity while traveling to visit even the smallest museum, for there may be an archaeological exhibit filled with gems of information about the history and prehistory of the region.

As noted earlier, these museums are only a sample of the many in existence (there are over 3000 museums in the United States alone). Some historical society museums are listed, but you will find others in your travels. Some college and university museums are listed, but almost every university, college, and junior college in the United States and Canada with an anthropology department has at least a small museum that houses an archaeological collection. Many archaeological sites, especially those that are part of a parks system in the United States and Canada, also have museums that are either on-site or nearby.

You can find out about these museums by contacting the state or province archaeologists or historical societies where you are planning to visit.

Some of the larger museums have special exhibits, and these are noted. Most large museums, however, have varied exhibits that cover a number of regions of the world. Regional museums generally have exhibits that are limited to finds from historical and prehistorical sites nearby. These are noted only if there are some special significance to the exhibits.

 ## Museums in the United States

American Museum of Natural History
Central Park West at 79th St.
New York, NY 10013
212–769–5650

Amerind Foundation
Dragoon, AZ 85609
602–586–3666

Black Hills Natural Sciences Field Station
South Dakota School of Mines and Technology
Rapid City, SD 57701
605–394–2494

Black Kettle Museum
PO Box 525
Cheyenne, OK 73628
405–497–3939

Bronson Museum
80 North Main St.
Attleboro, MA 02703
508–222–5470

This museum has exhibits of New England Amerinds.

California Academy of Sciences
Golden Gate Park
San Francisco, CA 94118
415–750–7145

California State Indian Museum
1218 K St.
Sacramento, CA 95814
916–324–0539

Charles D. Tandy Archaeological Museum
2001 Broadus, A. Webb Roberts Library
Southwestern Baptist Theological Seminary
PO Box 22417
Fort Worth, TX 76122
817–923–1921

Exhibits of early biblical periods, and artifacts from continuing expeditions at Tel Batash Timnah, Israel are housed in this museum.

Chisholm Trail Museum
605 Zellers Ave.
Kingfisher, OK 73750
405–375–5170

Cleveland Museum of Natural History
Wade Oval, University Circle
Cleveland, OH 44113
216–231–4600

Cobb Institute of Archaeology
Mississippi State University
Starkville, MS 39759
601–325–3826

Creek Council House and Museum
100 W. 6th
Okmulgee, OK 74447
918–756–2324

Cultural Heritage Center
2940 Singleton Rd.
Dallas, TX 75212
214–630–1680

The Center has local archaeological exhibits.

Denver Museum of Natural History
2001 Colorado Blvd.
City Park
Denver, CO 80205
303–370–6365

El Paso Centennial Museum
University and Wiggins Aves.
University of Texas at El Paso
El Paso, TX 79968–0533
915–747–5565

There is a good regional archaeology exhibit at this museum.

Field Museum of Natural History
Roosevelt Rd. & Lakeshore Dr.
Chicago, IL 60605–2496
312–922–9410

Fort Towson Historic Site
Rt. HC65, Box 5
Fort Towson, OK 74735
405–873–2634

Gilcrease Institute
1400 Gilcrease Museum Rd.
Tulsa, OK 74127
918–582–3122

Glenn A. Black Laboratory of Archaeology
9th and Fess Sts.
Indiana University
Bloomington, IN 47405
812–335–9544

The exhibits are devoted to the archaeology of the Great Lakes region.

Haffenreffer Museum of Anthropology
Brown University
Mt. Hope
Bristol, RI 02809
401–253–8388

This museum has extensive collections from North America.

Heard Museum of Anthropology and Primitive Art
22 East Monte Vista Rd.
Phoenix, AZ 85004
602–252–8848

Henderson Museum
University of Colorado
Boulder, CO 80309
303–492–8881

Horn Archaeological Museum
Andrews University
Berrien Springs, MI 49103
616–471–3273

Old World archaeology exhibits are housed at this museum.

Houston Museum of Natural History
1 Hermann Circle Dr.
Houston, TX 77030
713–526–4273

Hudson Museum
University of Maine
Orono, ME 04469
207–581–1901

Illinois State Museum
Spring and Edwards Sts.
Springfield, IL 62706
217–782–5964

Indiana State Museum
202 North Alabama St.
Indianapolis, IN 46204
317–232–4948

The Jewish Museum
1109 Fifth Ave.
New York, NY 10128
212–860–1889

This museum, operated under the auspices of the Jewish Theological Seminary of America, houses the only large collection of artifacts from Israel in New York City.

Kelsey Museum of Ancient and Medieval Archaeology
434 S. State St.
Ann Arbor, MI 48109
313–764–9304

Kerr Museum
Eastern Oklahoma Historical Society
PO Box 606
Poteau, OK 74953
918–647–8221

Lake Michigan Maritime Museum
Dyekman Ave.
PO Box 534
South Haven, MI 49090
616–673–8078

Underwater archaeology exhibits are the special focus of this museum.

Louisiana State Museum—Shreveport
3015 Greenwood Rd.
PO Box 9067
Shreveport, LA 71139
318–632–2020

Marine Museum at Fall River
70 Water St.
Fall River, MA 02722
508–674–3533

This museum has underwater archaeology exhibits.

Michigan Historical Museum
Michigan Library and Historical Center
717 West Allegan St.
Lansing, MI 48918
800–648–6630

This museum is also a source of information on other state historical museums, some of which have archaeological exhibits.

Montana Homeland
Montana Historical Society
225 North Roberts
Helena, MT 59620
406–444–2694

The Museum's exhibits go back over 12,000 years.

Museum of Geoscience
Old Geology Bldg.
Louisiana State University
Baton Rouge, LA 70803
504–388–2931

Museum of Natural History
Macbride Hall
The University of Iowa
Iowa City, IA 52242
319–353–8552

Museum of New Mexico
PO Box 2087
Santa Fe, NM 87504–2087
505–827–8941

Museum of Northern Arizona
Route 4, Box 720
Flagstaff, AZ 86001
602–774–5211

Museum of Primitive Culture
604 Kingstown Rd.
Peacedale, RI 02883
401–738–5711

The exhibits represent most major North American cultures, and many from other parts of the world.

Museum of the Big Bend
Sul Ross State University
Box C–120
Alpine, TX 79832
915–837–8143

This is a general history museum with archaeological exhibits.

Museum of the Great Plains
601 Ferris Avenue
PO Box 68
Lawton, OK 73501
405–581–3460

Museum of the Red River
812 SE Lincoln
Idabel, OK 74745
405–286–3616

Museum of the Western Prairies
1100 N. Hightower
PO Box 574
Altus, OK 73522
405–482–1044

Museum of Western Colorado
4th and Ute
Grand Junction, CO 81501
303–242–0971

Natural History Museum of Los Angeles County
900 Exposition Blvd.
Los Angeles, CA 90007
213–744–DINO

No Man's Land Historical Museum
Panhandle State University Campus, Sewell St.
PO Box 278
Goodwell, OK 73939
405–349–2670

Oklahoma Museum of Natural History
University of Oklahoma
1335 South Asp
Norman, OK 73019
405–325–4711

Old Sturbridge Village
Research Department
Sturbridge, MA 01566
508–347–3362

100th Meridian Museum
Main and Broadway
PO Box 564
Erick, OK 73645
405–526–3221

Peabody Museum of Natural History
170 Whitney Ave.
Yale University
New Haven, CT 06520
203–432–3730

Robert Lowie Museum of Anthropology
University of California
Berkeley, CA 94704
415–643–7648

San Diego Museum of Man
Balboa Park
San Diego, CA 92101
619–232–3821

Science Museums of Charlotte, Inc.
301 North Tryon St.
Charlotte, NC 28202
704–337–2639

South Street Seaport Museum
210 Front St.
New York, NY 10038
212–669–9424

This is one of the largest collections of urban archaeology open to public.

Southwest Museum of Science and Technology
State Fair Park
Dallas, TX 75226
214–426–3400

Spiro Mounds State Archaeological Park
Route 2, Box 339AA
Spiro, OK 74959
918–962–2062

State Museum of the Oklahoma Historical Society
2100 North Lincoln
Oklahoma City, OK 73105
405–521–2491

The Sydney L. Wright Museum
Jamestown Library
North Main Rd.
Jamestown, RI 02835
401–423–0436

This museum has prehistoric and Colonial artifacts from Conanicut Island.

Texas Baptist Historical Museum
Route 5, Box 222
Brenham, TX 77833
409–836–5117

This is a general history museum with archaeological exhibits.

Thomas Burke Memorial Washington State Museum
45th St. and 17th Ave., NE
Seattle, WA 98105
206–543–5590

Tomaquage Indian Museum
Nooseneck Hill Rd.—Arcadia
Richmond, RI
401–539–7213

This museum has archaeological collections from New England.

University Museum of Archaeology/Anthropology
University of Pennsylvania
Philadelphia, PA 19104
215–898–4000

University of Michigan Museum of Anthropology
4009 Ruthven Bldg.
Ann Arbor, MI 48109
313–764–0485

Western Trails Museum
PO Box 145
Clinton, OK 73601
405–323–1020

Wilderness Park Museum
2000 Transmountain Rd.
El Paso, TX 79999
915–755–4332

This is a museum devoted to archaeological and prehistorical exhibits.

Woolaroc Museum
PO Box 1647
Bartlesville, OK 74005
918–336–0307

 # Museums in Canada

Canadian Museum of Civilization
100, rue Laurier
Hull, QC J8X 4H2
Canada
819–776–7000

This museum has great exhibits of the native inhabitants of Canada.

Canadian Museum of Civilization
Metcalfe and McLeod Sts.
Ottawa, ON K1A 0M8
Canada
613–992–3497

Fort Dauphin Museum
PO Box 181
Dauphin, MB R7N 2V1
Canada
204–638–6630

Archaeological artifacts and archaeological laboratory are featured here.

Glenbow Museum
130 9th Ave., SE
Calgary, AB T2G 0P3
Canada
403–264–8300

Luxton Museum
  PO Box 850
  Banff, AB T0L 0C0
  Canada
  403–762–2388

Manitoba Museum of Man and Nature
  190 Rupert Ave. and Main St.
  Winnepeg, MB R3B 0N2
  Canada
  204–956–2830

Moncur Gallery of Prehistory
  Civic Centre
  Boissevain, MB R0K 0E0
  Canada
  204–534–2433

This museum has exhibits of the life of the people of the Turtle Mountain District prior to agricultural settlement.

Musée amerindien
  407, rue Amishk
  Mashteuiats, QC G0W 2H0
  Canada
  418–275–4842

The only Montagnais museum in Canada, it explores this ancient, native civilization.

Musée Arouane
  10, rue Alexandre-Duchesneau
  Wendake, QC G0A 4V0
  Canada
  418–845–1241

This is an ethnographic museum of Amerind cultural objects.

Musée d'archeologie
    2750, boul. des Forges
    Trois-Rivieres, QC G8Z 1V2
    Canada
    819–376–5032

The museum has exhibits on the evolution of man and society in the region.

Newfoundland Museum
    283–285 Duckworth St.
    St. John's, NF A1C 1G9
    Canada
    709–576–2460

Nova Scotia Museum
    1747 Summer St.
    Halifax, NS B3H 3A6
    Canada
    902–429–4610

Provincial Museum of Alberta
    12845 102nd Ave.
    Edmonton, AB T5N 0M6
    Canada
    403–427–1730

Royal British Columbia Museum
    675 Belleville St.
    Victoria, BC V8V 1X4
    Canada
    604–387–3701

Royal Ontario Museum
    100 Queen's Park
    Toronto, ON M5S 2C6
    Canada
    416–978–3692

Saskatchewan Museum of Natural History
Wascana Park
College and Albert
Regina, SK S4P 3V7
Canada
306–787–2815

University of British Columbia
Museum of Anthropology
6393 NW Marine Dr.
Vancouver, BC V6T 1W5
Canada
604–228–5087

 ## Museums Outside the United States and Canada

The museums listed are only a sample of museums around the world that have archaeological exhibits. You should contact the department of tourism for the countries you are interested in visiting to locate museums that have regional exhibits.

Bermuda Maritime Museum
PO Box MA 273
Mangrove Bay MA BX
Bermuda

Institute de Paleontologie Humaine
1 Rue René Panhard
75013 Paris, France
Tel. 43–31–62–91

This institution also sponsors a number of excavations that use volunteers.

Instituto Nacional de Antropologia e
Historia en Oaxaca
Pino Suarez 715
Centro. C.P. 6800
Oaxaca, Oaxoca, Mexico
Tel. 5–04–00

Israel Department of Antiquities and Museums
Ministry of Education and Culture
PO Box 586
91004 Jerusalem, Israel
Tel. 278–602/627

Museo Nacional Historia Nautral-Museo
Regional de Rancagua
Dr. Ruben Stehberg
Casilla 787
Santiago, Chile
Tel. 90011–45

Archaeological Sites

The sites listed below are a sampling of the many around the world, and are ones that have been advertised as open to visitors and/or volunteers in recent years. However, some may have completed excavations and closed access to the site. It is always best to call or write for confirmation before making a long trip to view a particular site. If a site has an established visitor center and/or museum it is more likely to be open for visitors throughout the year, and is not likely to have closed because the excavation is completed.

Although a number of the sites are listed as accepting volunteers, you should never expect to be accepted on the spot. Always make prior arrangements for any volunteer effort so that both you and the project director can be prepared. Volunteers are more likely to be accepted at the sites listed in the Excavations section that follows.

Most state and province park systems, as well as several federal agencies, administer archaeological sites, and information about sites not listed below can be obtained from agencies for various regions. An example of this is the Texas Parks and Wildlife Department (4200 Smith School Road, Austin, TX 78744; 800–792–1112), which administers many archaeological sites, including Seminole Canyon State Historical Park near Comstock, where excavations have uncovered the longest continuous story of humans in Texas; Hueco Tanks State Historical Parks near El Paso, where both historic and prehistoric pictographs have survived; Caprock Canyons State Park in the Panhandle region, where evidence of both Folsom and Plainview cultures have been discovered, and the Caddoan Mounds State Historic Site near Alto, where years of excavation work have uncovered thousands of artifacts.

 Sites in the United States

Alibates National Monument
  % Lake Meredith National Recreation Area
  PO Box 1438
  Fritch, TX 79036
  806–857–3151

This is a prehistoric flint quarry and ruins of Indian villages.

Angel Mounds State Memorial
  8215 Pollack Ave.
  Evansville, IN 47715
  812–853–3956

This is an excavated and restored Middle Mississippian site.

Blennerhassett Island
% Blennerhassett Historical Park Commission
PO Box 283
Parkersburg, WV 26102

This site near Parkersburg has both historic and prehistoric components, and is reached by a sternwheel boat. Volunteers are accepted by prior arrangement.

Caddoan Mounds State Historical Site
Route 2, Box 85C
Alto, TX 75925
409–858–3218

This prehistoric site has considerable excavation work completed.

Cahokia Mounds State Historic Site
PO Box 681, Collinsville Rd.
Collinsville, IL 62234
618–346–5160

Extensive excavation work has been done on mounds at this site, which has a museum and visitors' center.

Caprock Canyons State Park
PO Box 204
Quitaque, TX 79255
806–455–1492

This is an archaeological exhibit of excavations that uncovered evidence of the Folsom and Plainview cultures.

Center for American Archaeology
Kampsville Archaeological Center
PO Box 365
Kampsville, IL 62053
618–653–4395

This is a permanent archaeological research and teaching facility at the site of a 12,000-year-old site in the lower Illinois River Valley. You must make an appointment to visit the site. Amateur archaeologists may volunteer here by prearrangement.

Crow Canyon Center for Southwestern Archaeology
23390 Country Road K
Cortez, CO 81321
303–565–8975

This is a permanent archaeological research and teaching facility at an Anasazi pueblo site in southwestern Colorado. Visitors are welcome, and amateur archaeologists may work on the excavation by arrangement.

Crystal River State Archaeological Site
3400 North Museum Pt.
Crystal River, FL 32629
904–795–3817

No appointment is necessary to visit this prehistoric burial and ceremonial site that has a museum.

Curles Plantation Complex
% VCU–ARC
312 North Shafer St.
Richmond, VA 23284
804–367–8822

No appointment is necessary to visit the excavations of this early plantation on the James River, 17 miles east of Richmond on State Route 5. Volunteers are accepted with advance arrangement.

Dickson Mounds Museum
Lewiston, IL 61542
309–547–3721

This site has extensive excavations that have been completed, and an on-site museum.

Dogan Point Shell Midden
% Department of Anthropology
Appalachian State University
Boone, NC 28608

Located on the Hudson River just north of New York City, this site is the oldest mound on the Atlantic coast north of Panama. No appointment is necessary to visit the site, but is for a guided tour. Volunteers are accepted for work on the excavation.

Edge of the Cedars Ruin
% Winston Hurst
PO Box 788
660 West 400 North
Blanding, UT 84511
801–678–2238

This site is a small Anasazi village that has been partially excavated and reconstructed. Signs in downtown Blanding direct visitors to the site.

Effigy Mounds National Monument
PO Box K
McGregor, IA 52157
319–873–2356

Two hundred burial mounds and 26 earthen effigy mounds of the Red Ocher-Hopewell periods with on-site museum.

Elden Pueblo
% Coconino National Forest
2323 East Greenlaw Lane
Flagstaff, AZ 86004
602–527–7410

This pueblo site with 65 rooms is being stabilized and re-excavated as a participatory project using fourth through ninth graders, family groups, and amateur archaeology organizations. Visitors are welcome.

Fort Drum
℅ Jefferson County Historical Society
228 Washington St.
Watertown, NY 13601
315–782–3491

This is the site of an Iroquoian village, and may be visited by arrangement with the historical society. Volunteers for the excavation should contact Andover Foundation for Archaeological Research, PO Box 83, 1 Woodland Drive, Andover, MA 01810; 508–470–0810.

Fort Michilimackinac
PO Box 377
Mackinaw City, MI 49701
616–436–5683

This is a restored military fort and French colonial trading town open to visitors.

Fort Wayne
6053 West Jefferson Ave.
Detroit, MI 48209
313–849–0299

This is an intact fort that dates from 1848 and that has two burial mounds from 1400 to 1100 B.P.

Grand Mound Center
℅ Michael Budak
Rte. 7, Box 453
International Falls, MN 56649
218–279–3332

This is a site with a large burial mound and an on-site museum.

Historic Fort Snelling
Fort Snelling History Center
St. Paul, MN 55111
612–726–1171

This historic fort has been restored and reconstructed. Visitors are welcome, but no work is currently available to volunteers.

Historic St. Mary's City
Department of Research
St. Mary's City, MD 20686
301–862–0974

This was the founding site of the Maryland colony in 1634, but all traces of the city had vanished by 1750. No appointment is necessary to visit the site from June through August. Volunteers are accepted by prior arrangements.

Homolovi Ruins State Park
Park Manager
State Park Office
523 West Second St.
Winslow, AZ 86047
602–289–4106

This is Arizona's first archaeological state park, and is composed of six separate sites that have pueblos ranging in size from 10 to 800 rooms. Volunteers are accepted for a variety of positions in the park, and volunteers for the excavation should apply to Earthwatch, 680 Mount Auburn St., PO Box 403, Watertown, MA 02172; 617–926–8200.

Huntsville Mounds
% Department of Anthropology
University of Arkansas
Fayetteville, AR 72701
501–575–2508

This site near Huntsville includes at least four large earthen mounds from a late prehistoric Caddoan civic-ceremonial center. An appointment is necessary to visit the site, and volunteers are accepted.

Indian Mound Park
% Blanchard Chamber of Commerce
Blanchard, MI 49310

These two conical burial mounds are located near the intersection of Blanchard and Coldwater Roads in the hamlet of Rolland Center, 4 miles east of Blanchard.

Isle Royal Copper Pits
Isle Royal National Park
Houghton, MI 49931

These prehistoric copper pits were mined by Indians about 5000 B.P. They are accessible only by foot, and involve a rugged hike.

Lubbock Lake National Historic Landmark
% Dr. Eileen Johnson
The Museum of Texas Tech University
Lubbock, TX 79409

This is a stratified archaeological site containing the full complement from Paleoindian to historic period occupations.

Mitchell Prehistoric Indian Village
PO Box 621
Indian Village Road
Mitchell, SD 57301
605–996–5473

This is the only national archaeological landmark in South Dakota open to the public year round. It is a fortified Plains Indian village dating from the eleventh century with an on-site museum, a walk-through lodge which has been recreated for visitors, and a visitor center. No appointment is necessary to visit the site, and volunteers are accepted.

Mound City Group National Monument
16062 State Route 104
Chillicothe, OH 45601
614–774–1125

This is a Hopewell burial ground with 23 mounds and an on-site museum.

Mound State Monument
PO Box 66
Moundville, AL 35474
205–348–7774

This site was the seat of a Mississippian Stage chiefdom between A.D. 1000 and A.D. 1450, and has over 20 mounds. The site is open to visitors without an appointment, and volunteers are accepted by prior arrangement.

Norton Mounds
Grand Rapids Public Museum
54 Jefferson, SE
Grand Rapids, MI 49503
616–456–3977

This is a Hopewellian site with artifacts from the excavation on display in the Grand Rapids Public Museum.

Old Fort Niagara
PO Box 469
Youngstown, NY 14174
716–745–9667

This is a restored fort near the mouth of the Niagara River. Underwater surveys have been done nearby, and volunteers are accepted for excavation work.

Old Stone Fort State Archaeological Area
Route 7, PO Box 7400
Manchester, TN 37355
615–728–0751

This ceremonial enclosure dates from about 2000 B.P. Visitors are welcome without appointments.

Pinson Mound State Archaeological Area
460 Ozier Road
Pinson, TN 38366
901–988–5614

This is the largest site of its type in the Southeast. It has 12 mounds, a circular embankment, and an associated habitation site. Visitors are welcome without appointments, and volunteers are accepted under special conditions.

Pot Creek Pueblo
% Fort Burgwin Research Center
PO Box 300
Ranchos de Taos, NM 87557
505–758–8322

Directions to this 300-room multi-story pueblo can be obtained from the Fort Bergwin Research Center. An appointment is necessary to visit the site.

Poverty Point
% Geosciences Department
Northeast Louisiana University
Monroe, LA 71209–0550

This is one of the earliest major settlements in North America, and dates back almost 5000 B.P. It is located off State Route 577 north of Epps. No appointment is necessary for visitors, and volunteers are accepted.

Rock Creek Station State Historic Park
PO Box 36, Route 4
Fairbury, NE 68352
402–729–5777

This site was occupied from 1857 to 1867 as a Pony Express station and stage stop on the Oregon Trail.

San Luis Archaeological and Historic Site
202 West Mission Rd.
Tallahassee, FL 32303–1624
904–487–3711

This site has a field school, museum, and extensive educational components.

Seminole Canyon State Historical Park
PO Box 820
Comstock, TX 78837
915–292–4464

This is a prehistorical and historical site that has exhibits and a visitors' center. Rock shelters and art are also found in adjoining Amistad National Recreation Area, but are only accessible by boat.

Sonotabac Prehistoric Indian Mound and Museum
2401 Wabash Ave.
Vincennes, IN 47591
812–882–7679

The site includes a cermonial mound of the Hopewellian culture from about 2300 B.P. and a museum.

Spiro Mounds
PO Drawer 217
Spiro, OK 74959
405–325–7246

These are burial mounds of Caddoan culture (A.D. 700 to A.D. 1450).

Toltec Mounds Archaeological State Park
#1 Toltec Mounds Rd.
Scott, AR 72142–9502
501–961–9442

This is the largest prehistoric site in Arkansas, and has a visitor center and exhibits. It is 15 miles southeast of Little Rock. Volunteers are accepted through the Arkansas Archaeological Society, PO Box 1222, Fayetteville, AR 72702.

Ute Mountain Tribal Park
Towoas, CO 81334
303–565–8548

The Johnson Canyon pueblo ruins of the Anasazis, who lived in the area about 1600 B.P. can be viewed on guided tours of one to four days. The ruins are near the more famous Mesa Verde Ruins National Monument. Tour arrangements must be made in advance.

Wickliffe Mounds
PO Box 155
Wickliffe, KY 42087
502–335–3681

This site from the Mississipian Period overlooks the Mississippi River, and has shelters covering the open excavation areas. It is open to visitors without an appointment, and volunteers are accepted.

 ## Sites in Canada

Camp Rayner Site
℅ Saskatchewan Archaeological Society
#5–816 1st Avenue North
Saskatoon, SK S7K 1Y3
Canada
306–664–4124

This site, 4½ miles east and 3½ miles south of Birsay, is a large one where materials establish inhabitation back at least 5000 years. Indications are that excavations will date the occupation back 10,000 to 11,000 years. No appointment is required for visitors during the excavation season, generally July. Volunteers are accepted through the society.

The Enclosure Park
% Director, Archaeology Branch, Culture Division
Department of Tourism, Recreation, and Heritage
PO Box 6000
Fredericton, NB E3B 5H1
Canada
506–622–0761

This site is located just southwest of Newcastle in northeastern New Brunswick, and includes an eighteenth century French battery, an Acadian refuge area, and a Scottish settlement, as well as signs of later occupations. Visitors are welcome, and volunteers are accepted.

Fort McLeod Historic Park
% Heritage Properties North
Barkerville, BC V0K 1B0
Canada
604–994–3332

This is the site of the first trading post for the Northwest Company west of the Rocky Mountains, and is located on B.C. Highway 97, north of McLeod Lake. An appointment is necessary to visit the site.

Jones Site
Huronia Museum
Little Lake Park
PO Box 638
Midland, ON L4R 4P4
Canada

This is an undisturbed and unplowed Huron Indian village near the Huronia Museum. Write to the museum for an appointment to visit the site with a guide. Some volunteers are occasionally accepted on the excavation.

Kenosewun Visitor Centre and Museum
#1 Keystone Dr.
Selkirk, MB R1A 2H5
Canada
204–945–6784

This is an important archaeological site at the St. Andrew's Rapids on the Red River.

L'Anse Meadows National Historic Park
PO Box 70
St. Lunaire-Griquet, NF A0K 2X0
Canada
709–623–2601

The site of the earliest known European settlement in the New World, established around the year 1000 A.D. by radio carbon dating, L'Anse Meadows is on the Great Northern Peninsula of Newfoundland.

Manitoba Museum of Man and Nature
190 Rupert Ave.
Winnepeg, MB R3B 0N2
Canada
204–956–2830

Contact the above for information about archaeological sites in Manitoba. These include Grand Valley Park, on Hwy. 1, 10 kilometers west of Brandon; The Manitoba Escarpment, near Carman; Ice Age Remnants, near Milner Ridge; Bannock Point, between Nutamik and Betula Lakes; Whiteshell Provincial Park, and The Forks in downtown Winnepeg.

Nestor Falls Site
% Archaeological Field Office
Ministry of Culture and Communications
2nd Floor, 227 2nd St., South
PO Box 2880
Kenora, ON P9N 1X8
Canada

This is a stratified village site that covers an extended period. It is located between Fort Frances and Kenora in southern Ontario. Visitors and volunteers are welcome.

Port au Choix National Historic Park
% L'Anse aux Meadows National Historic Park
PO Box 70
St. Lunaire-Griquet, NF A0K 2X0
Canada
709–623–2601

Port au Choix NHP is located in Port au Choix, NF on the Great Northern Peninsula, and is the site of the burial ground of the Maritime Archaic Indians more than 8000 B.P.

Signal Hill National Historic Park
PO Box 5879
St. John's, NF A1C 5X4
Canada
709–772–5367

A visitors' center, gun batteries, and nineteenth century military buildings are all open for visitors.

Site archeologique de las Pointe-du-Buisson
33, rue Emond
Melochville, QC J0S 1J0
Canada
514–429–7857

This is a site that was inhabited for 5000 years by the Autochthonous. It is now an archaeological municipal park.

Strathcona Site
% Department of Archaeology
University of Calgary
Calgary, AL T2N 1N4
Canada
403–220–5227

This site, on 17th Street south of Highway 16 in Calgary, is a large campsite that dates back about 4500 B.P. The excavation and visitors' center are open to public, and volunteers are accepted on the excavation with advance approval.

Toronto Historical Board
Stanley Barracks
Exhibition Place
Toronto, ON M6K 3C3
Canada
416–392–6827

Fort York was the founding spot of Toronto in 1793. An ongoing excavation and restored buildings are open to the public.

Vieux-Poste
Boulevard des Montagnais
Sept-Iles, QC G4R 1X7
Canada
418–968–2070

A historical archaeological excavation helped reconstruct the Vieux-Poste according to eighteenth century plans.

Voutes du Palais
8, rue Valliere
Quebec, QC
Canada
418–691–6092 or 418–691–6285

Write or call the above to take a tour of a historical archaeological excavation.

Sites Outside the United States and Canada

Aizanoi
% The German Archaeological Institute
Cumus suyu
Ayarpaza Camii
Sokak 48
Istanbul, Turkey

This site, located in ancient Phrygia near Kutahya, was a Roman town during the reign of Hadrian. No appointment is necessary to visit.

Ayanis
E.U. Edebiyat Fak
Bornova-izmir, Turkey
Tel. 90–51–181101

This site is on Lake Van about 25 miles north of the city of Van, and was a Urartian fortress about 2900 B.P. No appointment is necessary to visit during the summer.

Caerleon
Roman Legionary Museum
High Street
Caerleon, Gwent NP3 1AE
Wales
Tel. 0633–423134

A completely excavated Roman amphitheater, fortress baths, barracks, and sections of the fortress walls are open to visitors. Other excavations are ongoing.

Castelo de Mertola
Campo Arqueologico de Mertola
7750 Mertola, Portugal

Remains from the Roman era through the Islamic occupation are preserved here. No appointment is needed to visit.

Castelo de Moura
Camara Municap de Moura
7860 Moura, Portugal
Fax 23602

Excavations explore extensive medieval and Islamic building sites. No appointment is necessary to visit the site.

Castro de Monte Mozinho
Museu Municipal de Penafiel
4560 Penafiel, Portugal
Tel. 055–23760

A late Iron Age hill fort excavation has revealed several Roman and pre-Roman occupations. An appointment is necessary to visit the site.

Castro de Santa Luzia
% Director of the Servico Regional de Arqueologia da Zona Norte
Apartado 250
4703 Braga codex, Portugal
Tel. 053–28051

This site near Viana do Castelo was a Celtic hill fort that was later occupied by the Romans. An appointment is necessary to visit the site.

Celje and Sempeter v Savinjski dolini
Pokrajinski musej
6300 Celje
Musejskitrg 1, Yugoslavia
Tel. 063–21–754

The town of Celje is located on top of the remains of an old Roman city. An archaeological park is located just outside town, and has Roman grave monuments dating from second and third centuries A.D. No appointment is necessary to visit the site, and volunteers are accepted.

Cerro Grande de la Compania
% Ruben Stehberg
Casilla 787
Santiago, Chile
Tel. 90011–45

This site is the largest fortress in the Cachapoal Valley, and was occupied by both the Inca and Promaucaes people 400 to 600 B.P. Appointments are necessary for visitors, and volunteers who are enrolled in, or graduates of, archaeology programs are accepted.

Chedworth Roman Villa
% The National Trust
Chedworth Roman Villa
Yanworth, Cheltenham
Gloucestershire GL54 3LJ, England
Tel. 024–289–256

This is one of the most intact Roman villas open to visitors in the United Kingdom. Visitors are welcome.

Choquepugio
% Arminda Gibaja Oviedo
Urbanizacion Mariscal Gamarra
B–3–415 2da etapa
Cuzco, Peru
Tel. 228714

A permit from the Instituto Nacional de Cultura and the site director is necessary to visit this excavation 18 miles outside Cuzco. A few volunteers are accepted each season.

Citania de Sanfins
% Museu Arqueologico da Citania de Sanfins
4590 Pacos de Ferreira, Portugal
Tel. 055–963897

One of the most important archaeological sites on the Iberian peninsula, this old fortification includes more than ten acres. It is about nine miles from Pacos de Ferreira, and no appointment is needed to visit.

Cressing Temple
% Mr. N. Brown
Cressing Temple Farmhouse
Cressing Near Braintree
Essex CM7 8PD, England
Tel. 0376–83220

This site was a major property of the Knights Templar, an order from the Crusades, and dates from about 800 B.P. No appointment is necessary on weekends between May and September; one is necessary all other times. Volunteers are accepted.

Dundee Bay Site
% Julian Granberry
PO Box 398
Horseshoe Beach, FL 32648

This site is a Lucayan village located on the south coast of Grand Bahama Island. One of the largest open-air village sites ever located in the Bahamas, it will have an ongoing excavation for the next five or six years. Volunteers over 21 years of age are accepted.

El Balneario
% Nestor Kriscautzky
Casilla de Correos 468
4700 Catamarca, Argentina

Many archaeological periods are represented at this site on the outskirts of Catamarca. Details about visits and volunteer opportunities can be obtained from the contact person listed above.

Freixo
Gabinete da Area Arqueologica de Freixo
4630 Marco de Canaveses, Portugal
Tel. 02–6000095

This site on the road from Marco de Canaveses to Regua is an extensive one with evidence of both Roman and pre-Roman occupation. An appointment is needed to visit.

Gordion
% Kenneth Sims
Department of Classics, CB #3145
212 Murphey Hall
University of North Carolina
Chapel Hill, NC 27599–3145

This site in Turkey has a history that spans from the Early Bronze Age into Roman times, and the excavations there belong primarily to the time of King Midas. It lies between the villages of Beylikkopru and Yassihoyuk southwest of Ankara. No appointment is necessary to visit the site.

Guayabo de Turrialba
% Horatio Rodriguez
Lasca Airlines
630 5th Avenue
New York, NY 10111
212–245–6370

The Universidad de Costa Rica has conducted a continuing excavation in this national park since 1978. Mounds, circular house foundations, aqueducts, and plazas have all been exposed and are open to visitors. Volunteers were not being accepted as of 1990, but were being considered for later.

Ikiztepe
% Onder Bigli
Akeoliji ve Sanat Tarihi B1.
I.U. Edebiyat Fakultesi
34459 Istanbul, Turkey
Tel. 520–75–40/230

This is an early Bronze Age site with many fine tools, weapons, and jewelry removed in past excavations. No appointment is necessary to visit the site, which is in the village of Ikiztepe.

Ljubjana
61000 Ljubjana
Mestni musej
Gosposka 15, Yugoslavia
Tel. 061–222–902

This site is located near one of the most important ancient mountain passes between the Mediterranean, Alpine, and Pannonic regions. An appointment is necessary for a guided tour, and volunteers are accepted.

Newark Castle
% John Samuels
6 Old Road North
Cromwell, Newark
Nottinghamshire NG23 6JE, England
Tel. 0636–821727

This castle was built in the middle of the twelfth century by Bishop Alexander of Lincoln. No appointment is necessary to visit the site, but is for a guide of the excavation.

Novo Mesto
Zavod za varstvo nar. kult. dedisnine
68000 Novo Mesto
Kidricev trg 3, Yugoslavia
Tel. 068–21–019

This is an Iron Age hill fort and graveyard. No appointment is necessary to visit, and volunteers are accepted.

Roman Town of Baetulo

Cap del Department d'Arqueologia del Museu de Badalona
Museu de Badalona
Placa Assemblea de Catalunya
1 08911 Badalona
Barcelona, Spain
Tel. 384–17–50

This site began as a walled city about 2100 B.P., and many Roman features have been excavated. No appointment is needed to visit.

Southampton, Lower High Street

% Museum of Archaeology
Tower House, Town Quay
Southampton SO1 1LX, England
Tel. 0703–220007

Stone houses of rich, medieval merchants are part of a large-scale excavation. The site is covered, and has gangways and platforms from which visitors can view work in progress. It is open during the summer.

Tombs of the Kings

% Cyprus Museum
Nicosia, Republic of Cyprus
Tel. 02303185

This site is within the tourist town of Paphos on the south-western coast of Cyprus. It was inhabited as early as the Chalcolithic period, and reached prominence in the Late Bronze Age. No appointment is necessary to visit, and volunteers are accepted.

Whithorn Priory
   The Whithorn Trust
   The Old Town Hall
   Whithorn, Wigtownshire DG8 8PB, Scotland
   Tel. 098–85–508

The earliest recorded Christian community in Scotland has been revealed by excavations. No appointment is necessary for visitors, and volunteers are accepted.

York Archaeological Trust
   1 Pavement Road
   York YO 1 2NA, England
   Tel. 0904–643211

York is famed for its medieval structures, and has many excavation sites. A reconstructed Viking townscape and an Archaeological Resource Center are special attractions.

Excavations

The excavations listed below are ones that often allow visitors, but are primarily interested in volunteers who can help with the actual work of the excavation. Visitors are more likely to need appointments to observe the work at these sites, but are also more likely to see ongoing excavations than at the sites listed in the previous section.

You should always contact the organizations sponsoring the excavation well in advance of the date you wish to volunteer or visit. This avoids any conflicts that may crop up, and assures that you will be able to either work on the site or observe others at work when you arrive.

Excavations in the United States

Beaver Pond Site
% Department of Anthropology
University of Alaska
3211 Providence Drive
Anchorage, AK
907–786–1397

This late prehistoric and early historic site has many fine remains, and is two hours south of Anchorage. Visitors are welcome. Volunteers must be over 18 years of age and physically fit.

Besh-Ba-Gowah Pueblo
% John Hohmann
1110 East Missouri, #200
Phoenix, AZ 85014
602–234–1124

Extensive excavation, stabilization, and reconstruction has been ongoing at this 200-room pueblo since 1981. No appointment is needed to visit the site. Volunteers are needed year round, must stay a minimum of five days, and must apply at least two weeks in advance.

Center for American Archaeology
Kampsville Archaeological Center
PO Box 365
Kampsville, IL 62053
618–653–4395

This is a permanent archaeological research and teaching facility at the site of a 12,000-year-old site in the lower Illinois River Valley. You must make an appointment to visit the site. Amateur archaeologists may volunteer here by prearrangement.

Chandler's Point/Emerald Necklace Parks Archaeological Survey
% City Archaeology Program
Environmental Program Room 805
Boston City Hall
Boston, MA 02201

An archaeological survey is being conducted of Boston's city parks, many of which contain prehistoric sites that date from 7000 B.P. An appointment is necessary to visit any of the sites. Volunteers must be over 16 and capable of physical work.

Chippewa National Forest
% Archaeological Outreach Program
204 Research Lab Bldg.
University of Minnesota—Duluth
10 University Dr.
Duluth, MN 55812
218–726–7154

This program is excavating several sites in Minnesota and Wisconsin, and the site in the Chippewa National Forest dates from about 10,000 B.P. through the late seventeenth century. Visitors do not need an appointment, but should contact the address above for directions to the site. Volunteers must provide their own camping equipment.

Crow Canyon Center for Southwestern Archaeology
23390 Country Road K
Cortez, CO 81321
303–565–8975

This is a permanent archaeological research and teaching facility at an Anasazi pueblo site in southwestern Colorado. Visitors are welcome, and amateur archaeologists may work on the excavation by arrangement.

Eaton Site
% Bill Engelbrecht
Anthropology Department
Buffalo State College
1300 Elmwood Ave.
Buffalo, NY 14222
716–878–6520

Located in West Seneca, New York, this site is a Late Proto-historic Iroquois village with some evidence of Archaic occupation. Volunteers are accepted, and visitors are welcome by appointment.

Gamanche Creek Site
% U.S. Army Corps of Engineers
215 North 17th St.
Omaha, NE 68102–4978
402–221–3070

This site, which is in the Lewis and Clark State Park east of Williston, ND, has been occupied continuously for the past 4000 years. No appointment is necessary to visit the site. Volunteers under 16 must be accompanied by an adult and arrangements must be made in advance.

Gungywamp Site
% Early Sites Research Center
Long Hill
Rowley, MA 01969

This site on the New London YMCA property in Groton dates back about 2700 B.P. and suggests native contact with Iron Age Europe approximately 1500 B.P. Volunteers should contact above for information. Visitors are welcome by appointment.

Henschel Site
% Archaeological Rescue, Inc.
PO Box 17767
Milwaukee, WI 53217
414–352–2515

This site on the shore of an ancient glacial lake is about 100 miles west of Milwaukee off I-43. The prehistoric and historic occupations there span over 11,000 years. Visitors need an appointment. Volunteers must have previous field experience.

Leake Site
% Department of Anthropology and Linguistics
University of Georgia
Athens, GA 30602
404–542–1458

This site has two earth mounds that have been partially leveled, and a village of a later period. Volunteers over 15 years of age are accepted, and visitors are welcome at the site.

Mount Independence State Historic Site
% Department of Anthropology
University of Vermont
Burlington, VT 05405–0168
802–656–3884

This is considered to be the most important historic site in Vermont, and was a major Revolutionary War fortification. It is located roughly five miles outside Orwell, Vermont. Volunteers are accepted through the above and must stay a minimum of two weeks. No appointment is necessary for visitors. They are also accepted through the Department of Science and Technology, Rensselaer Polytechnic Institute, Troy, NY 12180–3590, 518–276–8503.

Saint Augustine
% City Archaeology Program
Historic St. Augustine Preservation Board
PO Box 1987
St. Augustine, FL 32085
904–824–3355

Excavations are undertaken year round by the Board. Volunteers are welcome, but must take a training program. Visitors are welcome at the sites, which vary throughout the year.

Santa Elena
% Stephen Wise
Parris Island Museum
MCRD
Parris Island, SC 29905
803–525–3765

This site was colonized by the French Huguenots in 1562, and they were succeeded by the Spanish in 1566. It was later settled by the English. Most of the excavations at the site have been of the remains of the Spanish period. Visitors are welcome, and can get directions from the museum named above. Volunteers are accepted by the Institute of Archaeology and Anthropology, University of South Carolina, Columbia, SC 29208; 803–777–8170.

Tinsley Site
% Department of Behavioral Sciences
New Mexico Highlands University
Las Vegas, NM 87701
505–425–7511

This is a prehistoric settlement with the remains of a community, with surface and sub-surface rooms. Visitors must have an appointment, and volunteers should send a letter of inquiry to the above address.

Tubac Presidio
% Anita Cohen
53a South Alma School Rd.
Mesa, AZ 85202
602–965–4579

Tubac was founded in 1752 and is the oldest European settlement in Arizona. It is 20 miles south of Tucson on I–19. Appointments are necessary for visits. Volunteers over the age of 14 are accepted.

Wellfleet Bay Wildlife Sanctuary
% Massachusetts Audubon Society
PO Box 236
South Wellfleet, MA 02663
508–349–2615

Volunteers are accepted at this Indian midden dating from about 1500 B.P. that is located on Cape Cod Bay.

 # Excavations Outside the United States and Canada

Begrawia
% Antiquities Service
PO Box 178
Khartoum, Sudan

This site, 100 miles north of Khartoum, was the capital of the Late Meroetic Kingdom, and includes a number of features, including some 75 pyramids. Appointments are necessary to visit the site. Volunteers are accepted.

Castle Mall
% Norfolk Archaeology Unit
17 St. George's Street
Norwich NR3 1AB, England
Tel. 0603–762291

This is an urban excavation of a Saxon town and Norman castle in Norwich. No appointment is necessary to visit the site. Volunteers are accepted.

Chartres
% D. Joly
12 rue du Cardinal Pie
28000 Chartres, France
Tel. 37–21–35–65

This is an urban rescue archaeology project studying the development of Chartres from Roman to medieval times. Appointments are necessary to visit the sites. Volunteers must be 18 years of age, and agree to stay a minimum of three weeks. Room and board are provided for volunteers.

Chateau des Comtes Champagne
% Annie Renoux
Institute d'histoire
L'Universite du Mans
Route de Laval
Le Mans 72017 Cedex, France

This chateau was occupied from the tenth through the thirteenth centuries. An appointment is necessary for visits. Ten to twenty volunteers over 18 years of age are accepted each season.

Crannoga
% R.T. Farrell
331 Rockefeller Hall
Cornell University
Ithaca, NY 14853
607–255–7434

Crannoga is near Lough Lene, Ireland, and the periods represented at the site range from Mesolithic to medieval. The site involves extensive underwater excavation work in a survey of artificial, fortified islands. An appointment is necessary to visit the site. Volunteers are accepted, and those with scuba certification are given preference.

Croton
% Institute of Classical Archaeology
Wagener Hall 5–7
The University of Texas at Austin
Austin, TX 78712
512–471–5742

The neolithic site of Capo Alfiere is near Croton, Greece, and is an impressed-ware site. Appointments are necessary for visits. Volunteers need not have previous experience, but archaeological training is helpful and you must stay at least one month.

Czastkow Polski
% Lidia Magacz
5931 1/2 North Northwest Highway, #217
Chicago, IL 60631
708–631–3881

This site from the second and third centuries is located just south of Warsaw. No appointment is necessary to visit the site. Volunteers must be 18 years of age or older.

Dysart
% Department of Anthropology
Kroeber Hall
University of California
Berkeley, CA 94720
415–642–3391

This site, located in County Kilkenny, Ireland, includes ruins from the thirteenth, fifteenth, and seventeenth centuries. Visitors need an appointment. Volunteers are accepted, but must pay a share of the excavation costs.

Kasfiki, Kokotos, and Palaiopolis
% Martha Joukowsky
PO Box 1837
Brown University
Providence, RI 02912
401–863–3188

All of these sites are located in Corfu, Greece near the old harbor of ancient Corfu. No appointment is necessary to visit the sites. Volunteers should be at least college age. Those with special skills such as a facility for computers or fluency in a foreign language, as well as some knowledge of local customs, are preferred. Participants are housed in local apartments.

La Croix Verte, Antran
% Jean Pierre Pautreau
Le Bourg, chateau
Larcher, 86370 Vivonne, France

This Bronze Age site is located in western central France. No appointment is necessary to visit the site. Volunteers must be at least 18 years of age and stay at least 15 days. Applications must be submitted by May 31st.

Long Bay Site
% Science Museum of Charlotte, Inc.
301 North Tryon St.
Charlotte, NC 28202
704–337–2639

This island may be the site of Columbus's first landing in the New World. Excavations have yielded many artifacts from both pre- and post-contact periods. No appointment is necessary to visit the site during excavations, but the excavation dates vary from year to year. Volunteers participate in the costs of the excavations.

Malain-Mediolanum
% Louis Roussel
52 rue des Forges
21000 Dijon, France
Tel. 80–30–05–20

This is the site of a Gallo-Roman town that was destroyed in the third century and never reoccupied. An appointment is necessary to visit the site. Volunteers are accepted.

Monte Alban Project
% Instituto Nacional de Anthropologia e Historia en Oaxaca
Pino Saurez 715
Centro. C.P.
6800 Oaxaca, Oaxaca, Mexico

This city was supposedly built by the Zapotecs about 2500 B.P. Recent excavations have traced human habitation back to 11,000 B.P. Volunteers and students are accepted, but must pay all of their own expenses.

Oxford Area and Northamptonshire
% Director
Oxford Archaeological Unit
46 Hythe Bridge Street
Oxford OX1 2EP, England
Tel. 0865–243888

A number of sites in the region are being surveyed and excavated. Volunteers are accepted.

St. Helena Island Penal Establishment
% Warren Osnam
PO Box 42
Kenmore, Queensland Q4075, Australia

Both Aboriginal and colonial materials are found in this national park area near Brisbane. An appointment is necessary to visit. Volunteers must be at least 18 years of age and stay for at least four weeks. Lodging is provided.

Wade's Green Plantation
% Museum of Cultural History
University of California at Los Angeles
405 Hilgard Ave.
Los Angeles, CA 900024
213–825–1864

This excavation is of an eighteenth century cotton plantation in the West Indies. No appointment is necessary to visit the site during excavation dates. Volunteers are accepted by prior arrangement.

Zufriedenheit
  % Elizabeth Righter
  PO Box 4629
  St. Thomas, U.S. Virgin Islands 80803
  809–774–3320, ext. 160

The emphasis of this excavation is the land-use history of the area. There are both a prehistoric site and a later Dutch/Danish colonial plantation site under excavation. Volunteers should contact the address above for more information.

Field Schools

The field schools listed below are a few of the many that operate around the world each year. Many other state and provincial archaeological societies offer field schools on a periodic basis, as do junior college, college, and university archaeology departments. You can check out those in regions that you are interested in.

Most field school participants can obtain college credit for their work, even if the field school is not directly associated with, or operated by, a college or university. If you are interested in college credit for your work, check with the field schools you are interested in to see if credit can be obtained for participating in their projects.

Field school participants learn the basic techniques of archaeological excavation while participating in an ongoing project. The primary difference between working at a field school and working on a regular excavation is the amount of special instruction participants receive during their stay.

Many of these field schools operate in different locations each year, and you should contact them to find out where they are currently conducting excavations.

If there is no phone listed the organization requests that you contact them by mail.

 # Field Schools in the United States

Andover Foundation for Archaeological Research
1 Woodland Rd.
Box 83
Andover, MA 01810
508–470–0840

The field work takes place in the southwestern United States, Bolivia, and Belize.

The Archaeological and Historical Research Institute
PO Box 300
Corrales, NM 87048

Archaeological Rescue
Milwaukee Public Museum
PO Box 17767
Milwaukee, WI 53217
414–352–2515

Archaeology Research Program
Department of Anthropology
Southern Methodist University
Dallas, TX 75275

Archaeological Society of New Mexico
PO Box 3485
Albuquerque, NM 87110
505–299–7773

Arizona Archaeological Society Field School
2125 West Royal Palm Rd., #1087
Phoenix, AZ 85021
602–864–9619

Baltimore Center for Urban Archaeology
802 E. Lombard St.
Baltimore, MD 21202–4511
301–396–3156

California Institute for Peruvian Studies
9017 Feather River Way
Sacramento, CA 95826
916–362–2752

Center for American Archaeology
Kampsville Archaeological Center
PO Box 365
Kampsville, IL 62053
618–653–4395

This is a permanent archaeological research and teaching facility at the site of a 12,000-year-old site in the lower Illinois River Valley. You must make an appointment to visit the site. Amateur archaeologists may volunteer here by prearrangement. The field school offers a training program.

Central Michigan University
Department of Sociology, Anthropology, and Social Work
Mount Pleasant, MI 48859
517–774–3443

The work is on historical and prehistorical excavations on Beaver Island.

Chittenango Landing Canal Boat Museum
Lakeport Rd.
RD #2
Chittenango, NY 13037
315–687–7364
315–687–3844

✓ *The Cleveland Museum of Natural History*
Wade Oval, University Circle
Cleveland, OH 44106
216–231–4600, ext. 244

Colorado Archaeological Society
Program for Avocational Archaeological Certification
PO Box 36217
Denver, CO 80236

This program for members of CAS provides instruction in basic archaeological skills, as well as providing experience in field and lab work.

The Corporation for Jefferson's Poplar Forest
PO Box 419
Forest, VA 24551
804–525–1806

Crow Canyon Center for Southwestern Archaeology
23390 Country Road K
Cortez, CO 81321
303–565–8975

This is a permanent archaeological research and teaching facility at an Anasazi pueblo site in southwestern Colorado. Visitors are welcome, and amateur archaeologists may work on the excavation by arrangement. The field school offers a training program.

Cultural Heritage Council
PO Box 462
Cayucos, CA 93430
805–995–3076

This organization's excavation of a 10,000-year-old site is at Anderson Marsh State Park in Lake County, California.

Field School in Archaeology
Department of Anthropology
DH–05
University of Washington
Seattle, WA 98105
206–543–9604

Four Corners School of Outdoor Education
East Route
Monticello, UT 84535
801–587–2859
Outside Utah: 800–525–4456

Indiana State University
Dept. of Geography and Geology
Terre Haute, IN 47808
812–237–2263

The field school provides training in historic archaeology.

Iowa Archaeological Society
Eastlawn
The University of Iowa
Iowa City, IA 52242
319–335–2389

The Society offers a field school program each year in the week preceding Memorial Day.

Kansas Archaeology Training Program Annual Dig
Kansas State Historical Society
120 West 10th St.
Topeka, KS 66612
913–296–4780

Lake Superior State University
Arts and Letters Department
Sault Ste. Marie, MI 49783

The site is an excavation of the French Fort Repentigny.

Louisiana Archaeological Society
305 Hickory
Springhill, LA 71075–2633

Michigan State University
The Museum
East Lansing, MI 48824
517–353–7861

The program is conducting a survey along the St. Mary's River.

Museum of Cultural History
Archaeological Field School
55A Haines Hall
University of California at Los Angeles
405 Hilgard Ave.
Los Angeles, CA 90024

UCLA's program offers field schools at various sites around
the world.

Museum of the Rockies
Education Department
Montana State University
Bozeman, MT 59717
406–994–5257

Previous excavations have been conducted in southwestern
Montana on sites that date as much as 9400 B.P.

Nine-Mile Canyon School of Archaeology
% Department of Anthropology
Brigham Young University
700 SWKT
Provo, UT 84602
801–378–3058

Northern Ohio Archaeological Field School
Cuyahoga Community College
11000 Pleasant Valley Road
Parma, OH 44130
216–987–5492

This field school excavates both prehistoric Native American and historic nineteenth century archaeological sites in Cuyahoga Valley, Ohio.

Oklahoma Anthropological Society
PO Box 374
Leedey, OK 73654

The Society offers a nine-day field school each year around Memorial Day weekend. Write the Society for information.

Old Sturbridge Village
Archaeology Field School
Sturbridge, MA 01566
508–347–3362

Saginaw Valley State University
Department of Sociology
University Center, MI 48710
517–790–4492

The program provides training at prehistoric sites in Bay County, Michigan.

San Luis Archaeological and Historic Site
Museum of Florida History
Tallahassee, FL 32304
904–487–3655

Southern Illinois University
Contract Archaeology Program
PO Box 1458
Edwardsville, IL 62026–1458
618–692–2059

The program of the Cahokia Mounds Field School in Geoarchaeology is open to those over 16 years old, and no prior experience is needed.

Southern Utah State College
Archaeological Field School
Cedar City, UT 84720

Summer Field School
Department of Anthropology-Sociology
PO Box 2000
SUNY
Cortland, NY 13045
607–753–2485

This is a cooperative project with the National Park Service.

Thomas Jefferson Memorial Foundation
PO Box 316
Charlottsville, VA 22902
804–296–5245

Three Rivers Field School
% Jay Crotty
Start Route, PO Box 831
Sandia Park, NM 87047
505–281–2136

University of Pittsburgh Summer Field Training Program in Archaeology
Anthropology Department
University of Pittsburgh
Pittsburgh, PA 15213
412–826–5554

Western Michigan University
Department of Anthropology
Kalamazoo, MI 49008
616–383–4024

The University sponsors training programs at prehistoric sites in St. Joseph and Kalamazoo counties.

Wickliffe Mounds Research Center
PO Box 155
Wickliffe, KY 42087
502–335–3681

 ## Field Schools in Canada

Archaeological Resource Centre
℅ Danforth Technical School
840 Greenwood Avenue
Toronto, ON M4J 4B7
Canada
416–393–0665

The Centre's training takes place at excavation sites within the city of Toronto.

Sainte-Marie among the Hurons
℅ Isobel Ball
PO Box 160
Midland, ON L4R 4K8
Canada
705–526–7838

This is a simulated, late sixteenth century Huron site that was created as part of an educational program. Students between 11 and 20 years of age are accepted in the program. Volunteers with archaeological background and teaching ability who can volunteer for a length of time are welcome to apply.

Saskatchewan Archaeological Society Field School
#5–816 1st Avenue North
Saskatoon, SK S7K 1Y3
Canada
306–664–4124

The archaeological excavations are at Lake Diefenbaker near Birsay, Canada.

Stanley Barracks
Exhibition Place
Toronto, ON M6K 3C3
Canada
416–392–6907

 # Field Schools Outside the United States and Canada

Arbeia Roman Fort and Museum
Archaeological Field Officer
Baring Street
South Shields
Tyne and Wear NE33 2BB, England
Tel. 091–456–1369

Fenland Archaeological Trust
Flag Fen Excavations
Fourth Drove
Fengate
Peterbourough PE1 5UR, England
Tel. 0733–313414

Canterbury Archaeological Trust Limited
92A Broad Street
Canterbury
Kent CT1 2LU, England

Nahal Yattir—Israel
  % Steven Derfler
  Department of Religion
  Hamline University
  St. Paul, MN 55104
  612–641–2392

Newark Castle Trust
  6 Old North Road
  Cromwell, Newark
  Nottinghamshire NG23 6JE, England

Sutton Hoo Research Trust
  Sutton Hoo Research Project
  Sutton Hoo, Woodbridge
  Suffolk IP12 3DJ, England
  Tel. 30943–7673

York Archaeological Trust
  Excavations Coordinator
  1 Pavement
  York YO1 2NA, England
  Tel. 0904–643211, Ext. 238

Organizations That Assist with Placement of Volunteers

The following organizations all provide assistance to amateur archaeologists who wish to find excavations where they can actively participate in a dig. Some of the organizations are only concerned with archaeology, while others place volunteers in a wide variety of activities.

American Institute of Archaeology
675 Commonwealth Ave.
Boston, MA 02215
617–353–9361
Fax 617–353–6550

The Institute has lists of excavations in both the Old and New World where amateurs can visit and/or volunteer.

Andover Foundation for Archaeological Research
PO Box 83
Andover, MA 01810
508–470–0840

AFAR sponsors excavations in the southwestern United States, Belize, and Bolivia that include cave excavations, early Mayan villages, underwater archaeology of Little Spanish Armada, and early pottery and pre-ceramic surveys.

Archaeological Assistance Division
National Park Service
Interior Bldg.
PO Box 37127
Washington, DC 20013–7127
202–343–6843

Many archaeology projects of the NPS are directed by the division cited above, but others are operated by the regional offices listed below. You can contact the regions directly if you are interested in a particular area. Much of the archaeology work done by the NPS is historical archaeology at such places as national battlefields and monuments.

Regional Offices
North Atlantic
15 State St.
Boston, MA 02109
617–223–3769

Mid-Atlantic
143 S. Third St.
Philadelphia, PA 19106
215–597–7013

National Capital
1100 Ohio Dr., SW
Washington, DC 20242
202–426–6612

Southeast
75 Spring St., SW
Atlanta, GA 30303
404–221–5185

Midwest
1709 Jackson St.
Omaha, NE 68102
402–221–3431

Southwest
Old Santa Fe Trail
PO Box 728
Santa Fe, NM 87501
505–988–6388

Rocky Mountain
PO Box 25287
Denver, CO 80225
303–236–8700

Western
450 Golden Gate Ave.
PO Box 36063
San Francisco, CA 94102
415–556–4196

Pacific Northwest
1920 Westin Bldg.
2001 Sixth Ave.
Seattle, WA 98121
206–442–5565

Alaska
2525 Gambell St., Room 107
Anchorage, AK 99503
907–261–2690

Archaeology Abroad
31–34 Gordon Square
London WC1H 0PY, England

Archaeology Abroad does not run excavations, but publishes an annual bulletin (in March) and a bi-annual newsletter (Spring and Fall) that are available through subscription. These list projects and give detailed information about their staffing needs.

Chantiers D'Etudes Medievales
4, rue du Tonnelet Rouge
67000, Strasbourg, France
Tel. 88–37–17–20

The activity focus of this organization is restoration of medieval sites and monuments at Strasbourg and Viviers, France.

The Charleston Museum
360 Meeting St.
Charleston, SC 29403
803–722–2996

The Museum can provide information about archaeological excavations on urban homesites and rural plantations.

Club du Vieux Manoir
10, rue de la Cossonnerie
75001, Paris, France

This organization can direct you to work in restoration of ancient monuments and sites at three permanent locations—Guise, Argy, and Ponipoint, in addition to 12 to 15 other sites throughout France.

The Colonial Williamsburg Foundation
Department of Archaeological Research
PO Box C
Williamsburg, VA 23187
804–220–7330

Volunteers are welcome to do archaeological field and laboratory work at Williamsburg, Virginia, the eighteenth-century capital of the Virginia Colony.

Council for British Archaeology
112 Kensington Road
London SE11 6RE, England
Tel. 01–582–0494

The Council does not sponsor excavations but advertises projects in the *British Archaeological News*.

Crow Canyon Archaeological Center
23390 County Road K
Cortez, CO 81321
303–565–8975
800–444–8975

The Center can direct you to archaeology excavation and environmental archaeology projects in southwestern Colorado near Mesa Verde National Park.

Cultural History Council
PO Box 462
Cayucos, CA 93430
805–772–0117

The Council coordinates volunteer assistance for an archaeological excavation at a prehistoric site in Clear Lake Basin in northern California.

Division of Parks
Department of Natural Resources
Jobs Clearinghouse
State of Alaska
PO Box 7001
Anchorage, AK 99501

Most state park systems use amateur archaeologists on excavations, although Alaska is more active than most. Check with the state parks departments in the regions where you are interested in working to see if there are any excavations currently being conducted.

Dorset County Museum
High West St.
Dorchester, Dorset DT1 1XA, England

The Dorset Natural History Museum and Archaeological Society produces a list each spring of excavations taking place in Dorset throughout the spring, summer, and fall months.

Earthwatch Expeditions, Inc.
680 Mount Auburn St.
PO Box 403
Watertown, MA 02272
617–926–8200

Earthwatch sponsors professionally directed excavations in various regions of the world.

Foundation for Field Research
787 South Grade Rd.
Alpine, CA 92001

The Foundation sponsors professionally directed excavations, primarily in the New World.

Genqtur Turizm ve Seyahat Acentasi
Yerebatan Cad. 15/3 Sultanahmet
34410 Istanbul, Turkey
Tel. 90–1–526–54–09

This organization sponsors workcamps throughout Turkey, some of which are involved with archaeological excavations.

International Research Expeditions
140 University Dr.
Menlo Park, CA 94025
415–323–4228

This group sponsors scientific research projects around the world, some of which are in archaeology.

Israel Department of Antiquities and Museums
Ministry of Education and Culture
PO Box 586
91004 Jerusalem, Israel
Tel. 278–602–627

The Department publishes annually a list of excavations in Israel that use volunteers.

Kansas Archaeology Training Program
Kansas State Historical Society
120 West 10th St.
Topeka, KS 66612
913–296–4779

The Society provides information about archaeological excavations of prehistoric and historic sites, all in Kansas.

LA SABRANENQUE Restoration Projects
Saint Victor la Coste
30290 Laudun, France
Tel. 33–66–50–05–05
In the United States: 716–836–8698

You can be in contact with this group for information about restoration projects at several sites in southern France, in Saint Victor la Coste, near Avignon, and three sites in Italy.

Mount Vernon Ladies' Association
Archaeology Department
Mount Vernon, VA 22121
703–780–2000, Ext. 326

The Association provides volunteer coordination assistance for archaeological excavation and artifact processing projects at Mount Vernon, Virginia.

REMPART
1, rue des Guillemites
75004 Paris, France
Tel. 1–42–71–96–55

This organization will assist you in volunteering to help with archaeological restoration of historical monuments and sites of France.

RENAISSANCE du CHATEAU
77 Fir Hill Tower, Suite 9B2
Akron, OH 44304–1554
216–434–9362

Contact this organization to assist in the preservation of historic sites at various locations in France.

Service Archeologique du Musée de la Chartreuse
191, rue St-Albin
59500 Douai, France
Tel. 27–87–26–63, ext. 355

This sponsor of archaeological excavations at Douai, and Vitry-en-Artois, France, welcomes volunteer assistance.

Sierra Club Outings
Service Trips
730 Polk St.
San Francisco, CA 94109
415–981–8634

Although most of the service trips sponsored by the Sierra Club
are trail building and maintenance, the Club does offer a number of service trips that are involved with archaeological surveys.

Strathcona Archaeological Center Volunteer Program
Strathcona Archaeological Center, Strathcona Science Park
Edmonton, AL T6G 2P8
Canada
403–427–9487 or 403–422–5809 (May through September) and
403–220–7629 (October through April)

You can become a volunteer at the Archaeological excavations
of the Strathcona Archaeological Center, Edmonton.

Student Conservation Association, Inc.
PO Box 550
Charlestown, NH 03603
603–826–5206 or 603–826–5741

While this organization was formed to place students in a variety of outdoor and conservation jobs anyone is now accepted.
SCA places many volunteers in state and federal agencies that
conduct archaeological excavations and surveys.

United States Army Corps of Engineers
Office of the Chief of Engineers
20 Massachusetts Avenue, NW
Washington, DC 20314
212–272–0099

One of the responsibilities of the Civil Works division of the
Corps of Engineers is to preserve important historical and archaeological resources. Division offices of the Corps of Engi-

neers often have need of amateur archaeologists to help with archaeology projects, and they may be contacted directly. Address your correspondence to the Archaeologist, U.S. Army Corps of Engineers, followed by the specific address of the area of interest to you. You may also contact the archaeology volunteer coordinator at the above address.

Division Offices
New England
424 Trapelo Rd.
Waltham, MA 02254–9149

North Atlantic
90 Church St.
New York, NY 10007–9998

South Atlantic
510 Title Bldg.
Atlanta, GA 30335–6801

Ohio River
PO Box 1159
Cincinnati, OH 45201–1159

North Central
536 S. Clark St.
Chicago, IL 60605–1592

Lower Mississippi Valley
PO Box 80
Vicksburg, MS 39180–0080

Missouri River
PO Box 103, Downtown Station
Omaha, NE 68101–0103

Southwestern
1114 Commerce St.
Dallas, TX 75242–0216

North Pacific
PO Box 2870
Portland, OR 97208–2870

South Pacific
630 Sansome St.
San Francisco, CA 94111–2206

Pacific Ocean
Bldg. T–1
Shafter, HI 96858–5440

United States Bureau of Land Management
1849 C St., NW, Room 3615
Washington, DC 20240
202–208–5261

There are numerous archaeological sites and excavations on lands managed by the BLM, and many are coordinated and directed by BLM archaeologists. Amateur archaeologists are often used on BLM projects. For more information contact the BLM Volunteer Coordinator at the above address, or regional volunteer coordinators at the offices listed below.

Regional Offices
Alaska
222 W. 7th St., #13
Anchorage, AK 99513–7599
907–271–5076

Arizona
3707 N. 7th St.
PO Box 16563
Phoenix, AZ 85011
602–241–5501

California
Federal Office Bldg., Room E–2841
2800 Cottage Way
Sacramento, CA 95825–1889
916–978–4743

Colorado
2850 Youngfield St.
Lakewood, CO 80215
303–236–1721

Idaho
3380 Americana Terrace
Boise, ID 83706
208–334–1401

Montana
222 N. 32nd St.
PO Box 36800
Billings, MT 59107

Nevada
850 Harvard Way
PO Box 12000
Reno, NV 89520
702–328–6390

New Mexico
Joseph M. Montoya Federal Bldg.
South Federal Place
PO Box 1449
Santa Fe, NM 87504–1449
505–988–6030

Oregon
825 NE Multnomah St.
PO Box 2965
Portland, OR 97208
503–231–6251

Utah
324 South State St., Suite 301
Salt Lake City, UT 84111–2303
801–539–4010

Wyoming
2515 Warren Ave.
PO Box 1828
Cheyenne, WY 82003
307–772–2326

Eastern States
350 S. Pickett St.
Alexandria, VA 22304
703–461–1400

United States Forest Service
PO Box 96090
Washington, DC 20005–4788
202–447–3760

The USFS uses volunteers extensively in archaeological surveys and excavations. You can contact the USFS archaeologist at the above address, or regional archaeologists at the following regional offices listed below.

Regional Offices
Region 1, Northern
Federal Bldg.
PO Box 7669
Missoula, MT 59807
406–329–3316

Region 2, Rocky Mountain
11177 West 8th Ave.
PO Box 25127
Lakewood, CO 80255
303–236–9427

Region 3, Southwestern
Federal Bldg.
517 Gold Ave., SW
Albuquerque, NM 87102
505–476–3260

Region 4, Intermountain
Federal Office Bldg.
324 25th St.
Odgen, UT 84401
801–625–5669

Region 5, California
630 Sansome St.
San Francisco, CA 94111
415–556–4310

Region 6, Pacific Northwest
319 SW Pine St.
PO Box 3623
Portland, OR 97208
503–326–3625

Region 8, Southern
1720 Peachtree Rd., NW, Suite 800
Atlanta, GA 30367
404–347–4177

Region 9, Eastern
310 Wisconsin Ave.
Milwaukee, WI 53203
414–291–3612

Region 10, Alaska
Federal Office Bldg.
PO Box 21628
Juneau, AK 99802–1628
907–586–8752

University Research Expeditions Program (UREP)
PO Box L–3
University of California
Berkeley, CA 94720
415–642–6586

All of the archaeology expeditions sponsored by UREP are directed by archaeologists who are on the faculty of a branch of the University of California.

Upper Mississippi Valley Archaeological Research Foundation
2216 W. 112th St.
Chicago, IL 60643
312–239–1208 or 312–233–1711

This is an archaeological salvage and field school in central Illinois.

State Archaeologists and State Historic Preservation Officers

You can use this listing of state archaeologists and historic preservation officers to get information about the archaeological activities that are presently underway in each state. These offices generally have lists of archaeological sites that can be visited, museums that have archaeological exhibits, colleges and universities that are operating field schools and excavations, and rules and regulations governing antiquities in the state. Some have more information than others, and some states have very little archaeological activity.

The offices will also have a directory of archaeological and historical societies that are concerned with the history and prehistory of the region.

Alabama

State Archaeologist or **State Historical Preservation Office**
Alabama Historical Commission
725 Monroe St.
Montgomery, AL 36130
205–261–3184

Alaska

State Archaeologist or State Historic Protection Office
Division of Parks & Outdoor Recreation
PO Box 107001
Anchorage, AK 99510–7001
907–762–2622

American Samoa

State Historic Preservation Office
Director, Department of Parks and Recreation
Government of American Samoa
Pago Pago, American Samoa 96799
684–699–9614 or 684–699–9513

Arizona

Staff Archaeologist
Arizona State Museum
University of Arizona
Tucson, AZ 85721
602–884–2132 or 602–626–2556

State Historic Preservation Office
Arizona State Parks
800 West Washington, #415
Phoenix, AZ 85007
602–542–4009

Arkansas

State Archaeologist
Arkansas Archaeological Survey
PO Box 1249
Fayetteville, AR 72702–1249
501–575–3556

State Historic Preservation Office
    Arkansas Historic Preservation Program
    The Heritage Center, Suite 200
    225 East Markham
    Little Rock, AR 72201
    501–371–2763

California

State Archaeologist **or** *State Historic Preservation Office*
    Office of Historic Preservation
    PO Box 942896
    Sacramento, CA 94296–0001
    916–322–9623

Colorado

State Archaeologist **or** *State Historic Preservation Office*
    Colorado Historical Society
    1300 Broadway
    Denver, CO 80203
    303–866–2136

Connecticut

State Archaeologist
    Connecticut State Museum of Natural History
    U–23 University of Connecticut
    Storrs, CT 06269–3023
    203–486–5248

Staff Archaeologist, State Historic Preservation Office
    Connecticut Historical Commission
    59 South Prospect St.
    Hartford, CT 06106
    203–566–3005

Delaware

State Archaeologist
Bureau of Archaeology and Historic Preservation
15, The Green
PO Box 1401
Dover, DE 19903
302–736–5685

State Historic Preservation Office
Director, Division of Historical & Cultural Affairs
Hall of Records
PO Box 1401
Dover, DE 19903
302–736–5313

District of Columbia

State Archaeologist
Historic Preservation Office
614 H St., NW
Washington, DC 20001
202–727–7360

State Historic Preservation Office
1350 Pennsylvania Ave., NW
District Building
Washington, DC 20004
202–727–6365

Florida

State Archaeologist
Division of Historical Resources
Department of State
R.A. Gray Building
Tallahassee, FL 32399–0250
904–488–1480

Georgia

State Archaeologist
Room 208, Martha Munro
West Georgia College
Carollton, GA 30118–0001
404–834–6454

State Historic Preservation Office
Chief, Historic Preservation Section
Department of Natural Resources
205 Butler St., SE
Suite 1462
Atlanta, GA 30334–1703
404–656–2840

Hawaii

State Historic Preservation Office
Department of Land and Natural Resources
PO Box 621
Honolulu, HI 96809
808–548–6550

Idaho

State Archaeologist
Idaho Historical Society
210 Main St.
Boise, ID 83702
208–334–3847

Illinois

Chief Archaeologist and State Historic Preservation Office
Division of Preservation Services
Historic Preservation Agency
Old State Capitol Bldg.
Springfield, IL 62701
217–782–4836

Indiana

State Archaeologist
Department of Anthropology
Indiana University
Bloomington, IN 47405
812–337–1203

State Historic Preservation Office
Director, Department of Natural Resources
608 State Office Bldg.
Indianapolis, IN 46204
317–232–4200

Iowa

State Archaeologist
305 Eastlawn
University of Iowa
Iowa City, IA 52242
309–335–2389

State Historic Preservation Office or Archaeological Survey Program
Bureau of Historic Preservation
State Historical Society of Iowa
Capital Complex
Des Moines, IA 50319
515–281–8744

Kansas

State Archaeologist or State Historic Preservation Office
Kansas State Historical Society
120 West Tenth
Topeka, KS 66612
913–296–3251

Kentucky

State Archaeologist
Department of Anthropology
University of Kentucky
Lexington, KY 40506
806–564–7005

State Historic Preservation Office
Kentucky Heritage Council
Capitol Plaza Tower, 12th Fl.
Frankfort, KY 40601
502–564–7005

Louisiana

State Archaeologist or *State Historic Preservation Office*
Office of Cultural Development
PO Box 44247
Baton Rouge, LA 70804
504–342–8200

Maine

Research Associate, Archaeology
Maine State Museum
Augusta, ME 04333
207–289–2301

State Historic Preservation Office
Archaeologist, Maine Historic Preservation Commission
55 Capital St., Station #65
Augusta, ME 04333
207–289–2132

Maryland

State Archaeologist
Maryland Geological Survey, Division of Archaeology
2300 St. Paul St.
Baltimore, MD 21218
301–544–5530

State Historic Preservation Office
Director, Division of Historical and Cultural Programs
Dept. Of Housing and Community Development
45 Calvert St.
Annapolis, MD 21401
301–974–2150

Massachusetts

State Archaeologist
Massachusetts Historical Commission
80 Boylston St.
Boston, MA 02116
617–727–8470

Michigan

State Archaeologist or State Historic Preservation Office
Bureau of History
Michigan Department of State
Lansing, MI 48918
517–373–6362

Minnesota

State Archaeologist
Programs Office
Research Lab Building
University of Minnesota
Duluth, MN 55812
218–726–7154

Head, Archaeology Department
Minnesota Historical Society
690 Cedar St.
St. Paul, MN 55101
612–296–2747

Mississippi

Chief Archaeologist or *State Historic Preservation Office*
Director, Department of Archives and History
PO Box 571
Jackson, MS 39205
601–359–6850

Missouri

Senior Archaeologist
Historic Preservation Program
Missouri Department of Natural Resources
PO Box 176
Jefferson City, MO 65102
314–751–4422

Montana

State Archaeologist or *State Historic Preservation Office*
Historic Preservation Office
Montana Historical Society
225 North Roberts
Helena, MT 59620–9990
406–444–7715

Nebraska

Curator of Anthropology or *State Historic Preservation Office*
State Historical Society
PO Box 82554
Lincoln, NE 68501
402–471–3270

Nevada

Staff Archaeologist
State Historic Preservation Office
201 South Fall St.
Carson City, NV 89710
702–885–5138

State Historic Preservation Office
Director, Department of Conservation and Natural
Resources
Nye Bldg., Room 213
201 South Fall St.
Carson City, NV 89710
702–885–4360

New Hampshire

State Archaeologist or State Historic Preservation Office
Department of Libraries, Arts and Historical Resources
Division of Historical Resources
Walker Bldg.–15 South Fruit St.
Box 2043
Concord, NH 03302–2043
603–271–3483 or 603–271–3558

New Jersey

State Archaeologist
New Jersey State Museum
205 West State St.
Trenton, NJ 08625
609–292–8594

State Historic Preservation Office
Commissioner, Department of Environmental Protection
CN402
Trenton, NJ 08625
609–292–2023

New Mexico

State Archaeologist
Museum of New Mexico
PO Box 2087
Santa Fe, NM 87504
505–827–8941

State Historic Preservation Office
Historic Preservation Division
Office of Cultural Affairs
Villa Rivera, Room 101
228 East Palace Ave.
Santa Fe, NM 87503
505–827–8320

New York

State Archaeologist
Cultural Education Center
Room 3122
Albany, NY 12230
518–474–0444

North Carolina

State Archaeologist or State Historic Preservation Office
Division of Archives and History
109 East Jones St.
Raleigh, NC 27611
919–733–7305

North Dakota

Chief Archaeologist
Archaeology and Historic Preservation Division
State Historical Society of North Dakota
North Dakota Heritage Center
612 East Boulevard Ave.
Bismarck, ND 58505
701–224–2667

Ohio

Ohio Historic Preservation Office
Ohio Historic Society
1985 Velma Ave.
Columbus, OH 43211
614–297–2470

Oklahoma

State Archaeologist
Oklahoma Archaeological Survey
1808 Newton Dr., Room 116
Norman, OK 73019
405–325–7211

State Historic Preservation Office
Executive Director
Oklahoma Historical Society
Historical Bldg.
2100 North Lincoln
Oklahoma City, OK 73105
405–521–2491

Oregon

State Historic Preservation Office
State Parks Administrator
525 Trade St., SE
Salem, OR 97310
503–378–5019

Pennsylvania

Curator of Archaeology or Bureau of Historic Preservation
The State Museum of Pennsylvania
PO Box 1026
Harrisburg, PA 17108–1026
717–787–2891

Puerto Rico

State Historic Preservation Office
Office of the Governor
Box 82, La Fortalenza
San Juan, PR 00901
809–721–3737

State Archaeologist
Oficiana Estagatal De Preservacion Historica
La Fortalenza
San Juan, PR 00901
809–723–3012

Rhode Island

Rhode Island Historical Preservation Commission
Old State House
150 Benefit St.
Providence, RI 02903
401–277–2678

South Carolina

State Archaeologist
South Carolina Institute of Archaeology and Anthropology
1321 Pendleton St.
University of South Carolina
Columbia, SC 29208
803–777–8170 or 803–734–0567

State Historic Preservation Office
South Carolina Department of Archives and History
PO Box 11669
Columbia, SC 29211–1669
803–734–8577

South Dakota

State Historic Preservation Office
   Director, Office of History
   South Dakota State Historical Society
   900 Governors Dr.
   Pierre, SD 57501
   605–773–3458

State Archaeologist
   State Archaeological Research Center
   2425 East St. Charles St.
   Rapid City, SD 57701–5005
   605–394–1936

Tennessee

State Archaeologist
   Conservation Department
   Customs House
   701 Broadway
   Nashville, TN 37219–5237
   615–742–6607

Texas

State Archaeologist
   Texas Historical Commission
   PO Box 12276
   Capital Station
   Austin, TX 78711
   512–463–6090

Utah

State Archaeologist **or** *State Historic Preservation Office*
   Utah State Historical Society
   300 Rio Grande
   Salt Lake City, UT 84101
   801–533–5755

Vermont

State Archaeologist
Division for Historic Preservation
Pavilion Building
Montpelier, VT 05602
802–828–3226

Virgin Islands

DPRR
State Historic Preservation Office
Nisky Center, Suite 231
St. Thomas, VI 00802
809–774–7859

Virginia

State Archaeologist or State Historic Preservation Office
Virginia Research Center for Archaeology
Department of Historic Resources
221 Governor St.
Richmond, VA 23219
804–786–3143

Washington

State Archaeologist or State Historic Preservation Office
Department of Community Development
Archaeology and Historic Preservation
111 West 21st Ave., KL–11
Olympia, WA 98504–5411
206–753–4011

West Virginia

State Archaeologist
Blennerhassett Historical State Park
PO Box 283
Parkersburg, WV 26102
304–428–3000

State Historic Preservation Office
Commissioner, Division of Culture and History
Capitol Complex
Charleston, WV 25305
304–348–0220

Wisconsin

State Archaeologist
Division of Historic Preservation
State Historical Society of Wisconsin
816 State St.
Madison, WI 53706
608–262–1339

Wyoming

State Archaeologist
PO Box 3431–University Station
Laramie, WY 82070
307–766–5301

State Historic Preservation Office
Archives, Museums and Historical Department
Barrett Bldg.
2301 Central
Cheyenne, WY 82002
307–777–6311

Canadian Provincial Archaeological Units

Canadian provincial governments, as a rule, do not have specific and permanent government archaeologists. Since the addresses, and names, of provincial archaeologists change frequently, you should contact the agency below for current names and addresses of the provincial archaeologists for the regions you are interested in visiting.

Archaeological Survey of Canada
  Canadian Museum of Civilization
  100 Laurier St.
  POB 3100, Station B
  Hull, PQ J8X 4H2
  Canada
  819–994–6110

Governmental Agencies Outside the United States and Canada

Almost every country in the world has an agency that supervises the archaeological activities of both residents and visitors. You can contact consulates or embassies for the current address of the correct agency for the region you plan on visiting. This agency will give you information about the archaeological activities currently underway, and provide you with information about laws and regulations concerning archaeology and antiquities.

Archaeological Organizations

The organizations listed below are a sample of archaeological organizations. Many publish magazines, monographs, books, and other materials concerning ongoing activities in archaeology. Look for those that specialize in your areas of interest, and contact them about membership requirements.

Many of them also help amateurs locate excavations and field schools where they can work.

Those without phone numbers prefer to be contacted by mail.

American Academy in Rome
   41 East 65th St.
   New York, NY 10021
   212–517–4200

American Anthropological Association
   1703 New Hampshire Ave., NW
   Washington, DC 20009
   202–232–8800

American Archaeology Division
   15 Switzler Hall
   University of Missouri
   Columbia, MO 65211

American Association of Museums
   1225 I St., NW
   Washington, DC 20003
   202–544–2422

American School of Classical Studies at Athens (ASCSA)
   41 East 72nd St.
   New York, NY 10021
   212–861–0302

American Schools of Oriental Research (ASOR)
   4243 Spruce Street
   Philadelphia, PA 19104
   215–222–4643

The Archaeological Conservancy
415 Orchard Dr.
Santa Fe, NM 87501
505–982–3278

Archaeological Groups of Italy
Via Tacinto, 41
00193, Rome, Italy
Tel. 382–329

Archaeology Abroad
31–34 Gordon Square
London WC1H OPY, England

Association for Field Archaeology
% *Journal of Field Archaeology*
Boston University
675 Commonwealth Ave.
Boston, MA 02215
617–353–2357

Biblical Archaeology Society
3000 Connecticut Ave., NW
Suite 300
Washington, DC 20008
202–387–8888

Canadian Mediterranean Institute
541 Promenade Sussex Dr.
Ottawa, ON K1N 6Z6
Canada
613–238–2207

Center for Archaeological Investigations
Southern Illinois University
Carbondale, IL 62901
618–536–5529

Center for Archaeological Sciences
  University of Georgia
  110 Riverbend Rd.
  Athens, GA 30602

Center for Cave and Karst Studies
  Western Kentucky University
  Bowling Green, KY 42101
  502–843–4979 or 502–745–4555

Center for Prehistoric Archaeology
  R.D. #1, Box 414
  Spring City, PA 19475
  215–495–7459

Centro Camuno di Studi Preistoric
  25044 Capo di Ponte
  Valcamonica
  Brescia, Italy
  Tel. 0364–42091

Council for British Archaeology
  112 Kensington Road
  London SE11 6RE, England
  Tel. 582–0494

Desert Research Institute
  Social Sciences Center
  University of Nevada System
  PO Box 60220
  Reno, NV 89506
  702–673–7303

Eastern Sites Research Society
  Long Hill
  Rowley, MA 01969
  617–948–2410

Eastern States Archaeological Federation
Roger Moeller
PO Box 386
Bethlehem, CT 06751

Egypt Exploration Society
3 Doughty Mews
London WC1N 2PG, England
Tel. 242–1880

Flowerdew Hundred Foundation
1617 Flowerdew Hundred Rd.
Hopewell, VA 23860
804–541–8897

Friends of Archaeology
Center of Archaeology Research
University of Texas
San Antonio, TX 78285

Institute of Andean Studies
PO Box 9307–0307
Berkeley, CA 94709

Institute of Nautical Archaeology
PO Drawer AU
College Station, TX 77840–1170

Intercollegiate Center for Classical Studies in Rome
via Algardi 19
00152 Rome, Italy

Israel Department of Antiquities and Museums
Ministry of Education and Culture
PO Box 586
91004 Jerusalem, Israel
Tel. 278–602 or 278–627

L.S.B. Leakey Foundation
Foundation Center 1–7
Pasadena, CA 91125

New York Institute of Anthropology
34–15 94th St.
Jackson Heights, NY 11372

Prehistoric Society
Department of Archaeology
The University
Whiteknights
Reading RG6 2AA, England

Saskatchewan Archaeological Society
#5–816 1st Avenue North
Saskatoon, SK S7K 1Y3
Canada
306–664–4124

School for Field Studies
196 Broadway
Cambridge, MA 02139
617–497–9000

Schools of American Research
Box 2188
Sante Fe, NM 87501
505–982–3583

Society for American Archaeology
1511 K St., NW
Washington, DC 20005
202–638–6079

Society for Historical Archaeology
  Room 5020
  National Museum of American History
  Washington, DC 20560
  202–357–2058

Suggested Reading

M ost archaeological organizations and societies publish articles, manuals, monographs, and books about their special concentration in the field of archaeology. They also maintain bibliographies of material that cover their areas of interest. If the books and periodicals listed below do not cover the particular subjects that interest you, you can contact the appropriate organizations listed in Chapter 18 to see if they can assist you in finding specialized material.

 ## Periodicals Listing Fieldwork Opportunities

There are a number of periodicals that are either devoted entirely to archaeology, or regularly include articles on the subject. There are also periodic publications such as the *Archaeological Fieldwork Opportunities Bulletin* from the Archaeological Institute of America (AIA), 675 Commonwealth Avenue, Boston, MA 02215, which lists excavation opportunities for volunteers, field school students, and some paid positions throughout the world. There were almost 100 pages of listings in the 1990 edition. The bulletin also includes listings of institutions and organizations affiliated with AIA that also use volunteers. To order this publication, write to the address above for current price and membership information.

Similar publications can be ordered from Archaeology Abroad, 31–34 Gordon Square, London WC1H OPY, England, and the Council for British Archaeology, 112 Kensington Road, London SE11 6RE, England.

 ## Periodicals with Archaeology Articles

American Antiquity

This well-written publication for professionals and amateurs is a quarterly that only covers New World archaeology. Society for American Archaeology, 1511 K Street, NW, Washington, DC 20009.

American Journal of Archaeology

Published quarterly, the *American Journal of Archaeology*, with close to 4000 subscribers, is one of the most widely distributed scholarly journals devoted to archaeology in the world. It devotes its issues to the studies of art and archaeology of ancient Europe and the Mediterranean world, including the Near East and Egypt, from prehistoric to Late Antique. Archaeological Institute of America, 675 Commonwealth Avenue, Boston, MA 02215.

Archaeology

In print since 1948, *Archaeology* is a richly illustrated magazine with a circulation of close to 150,000. Articles, which are written by professional archaeologists for both the general public and the scholar, provide accounts of the latest discoveries in archaeology worldwide. Archaeological Institute of America, 675 Commonwealth Avenue, Boston, MA 02215.

National Geographic

Published by the National Geographic Society, this popular magazine frequently has articles on archaeological activities. National Geographic Society, 17th and M Streets, NW, Washington, DC 20036.

General Archaeology Books

The books listed below are general in content, and are useful as references to archaeology around the world. For more specific references, e.g., books on mound builders of the midwest, check the bibliographies of several of the books listed below or contact archaeological societies and organizations that are concerned with specific periods or regions.

In addition to these books, there are several series of archaeological guide books. *The Blue Guide* is an excellent series of guide books published by Ernest Benn Limited, London. Individual volumes cover various parts of Western Europe, including the Mediterranean. Facts on File Publications also has a series of reference books on the ancient world with titles such as *Atlas of Ancient America*, *Atlas of Ancient Egypt*, and *Atlas of the Greek World*.

Barker, P.A. *Techniques of Archaeological Excavations* 2d ed. New York: Columbia University Press, 1963.

Bass, George F. *Archaeology Beneath the Sea*. New York: Walker & Co., 1975.

Bass, George F. *Archaeology Under Water*. London: Thames & Hudson, 1966.

Braidwood, Robert J. *Archaeologists and What They Do*. New York: Franklin Watts, 1960.

Brennan, Louis. *Beginner's Guide to Archaeology*. Harrisburg, PA: Stackpole Books, 1973.

Daniel, Glyn. *A Short History of Archaeology*. London: Thames & Hudson, 1981.

Daniels, Steve and David Nicholas. *The Archaeology Workbook*. Philadelphia: University of Pennsylvania Press, 1982.

Darcy, William S. *Archaeological Field Methods: An Introduction*. Minneapolis: Burgess Publishing Co., 1981.

Dillon, B.D., ed. *The Student's Guide to Archaeological Illustrating*. Los Angeles: Institute of Archaeology, University of California at Los Angeles, 1981.

Fagan, Brian M. *In the Beginning: An Introduction to Archaeology* 4th ed. Boston: Little, Brown & Co., 1981.

Fleming, Stuart. *Dating in Archaeology: A Guide to Scientific Techniques*. New York: St. Martin's Press, 1977.

Greene, Kevin G. *Archaeology, An Introduction: The History, Principles, and Methods of Modern Archaeology*. Totowa, NJ: Barnes & Noble, 1983.

Hester, Thomas R., Robert F. Heizer, and J. Graham. *Field Methods in Archaeology* 6th ed. Palo Alto, CA: Mayfield Publishing Co., 1975.

Hole, Frank and Robert Heizer. *An Introduction to Prehistoric Archaeology*. New York: Holt, Rinehart and Winston, 1969.

Hume, Ivor N. *Historical Archaeology*. New York: Alfred A. Knopf, 1969.

Joukowsky, Martha. *A Complete Manual of Field Archaeology*. Englewood Cliffs, NJ: Prentice-Hall, 1980.

McHargue, George and Michael Roberts. *A Field Guide to Conservation Archaeology in America*. New York: J.P. Lippincott Company, 1977.

McIntosh, Jane. *The Practical Archaeologist: How We Know What We Know About the Past*. New York: Facts on File Publishers, 1986.

Muckleroy, Keith. *Maritime Archaeology*. Cambridge & New York: Cambridge University Press, 1978.

Peterson, Mendel. *History Under the Sea*. Washington, DC: Smithsonian Institution, 1965.

Robbins, Maurice and Mary B. Irving. *The Amateur Archaeologist's Handbook*. New York: Thomas Crowell, 1965.

Sande, Theodore. *Industrial Archaeology*. Brattleboro, VT: The Stephen Green Press, 1976.

Sullivan, G. *Discover Archaeology: An Introduction to the Tools and Techniques of Archaeological Fieldwork.* New York: Penguin Books, 1980.

Wendorf, Fred. *A Guide to Salvage Archaeology.* Albuquerque, NM: Museum of New Mexico Press, 1966.

Wilkes, Bill. *Nautical Archaeology.* New York: Stein & Day, 1971.

Willey, Gordon R. and Jeremy Sabloff. *A History of American Archaeology.* San Francisco: W.H. Freeman and Co., 1974.

Willey, Gordon R. *An Introduction to American Archaeology*, Vol. 1. Englewood Cliffs, NJ: Prentice-Hall, 1980.

Wilson, David. *The New Archaeology.* New York: Alfred A. Knopf, 1975.

Wood, Robert. *A Travel Guide to Archaeological Mexico.* New York: Hastings House, Publishers, 1979.

Index